PERSUASION

PERSUASION

Getting to the Other Side

JOSEPH WILLIAM SINGER

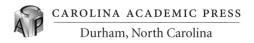
CAROLINA ACADEMIC PRESS
Durham, North Carolina

Library of Congress Cataloging-in-Publication Data

Names: Singer, Joseph William, 1954 author.
Title: Persuasion : getting to the other side / by Joseph William Singer.
Description: Durham, North Carolina : Carolina Academic Press, LLC,
    2019.
Identifiers: LCCN 2019032697 | ISBN 9781531012250 (paperback) |
    ISBN 9781531012267 (ebook)
Subjects: LCSH: Law-—United States. | Persuasion (Rhetoric) |
    Forensic oratory. | Legal composition.
Classification: LCC KF380.S54 2019 | DDC 340/.14—dc23
LC record available at https://lccn.loc.gov/2019032697

Carolina Academic Press
700 Kent Street
Durham, North Carolina 27701
Telephone (919) 489-7486
Fax (919) 493-5668
www.cap-press.com

Printed in the United States of America

CONTENTS

ACKNOWLEDGMENTS

Many people have helped me with this book. Thanks and affection go to Martha Minow and Mira Singer for their support, wisdom, suggestions, and feedback. Mira Singer provided the best developmental editing I have ever had; this book is far better because of her. Research for this book was made possible by research grants from Harvard Law School. I also thank the Hagler Institute for Advanced Study at Texas A&M University and the William S. Richardson School of Law Frank Boas Visiting Professor fund for allowing me to be in residence at their respective law schools.

The idea of categorizing legal arguments and arranging them in argument-counterargument pairs was invented by Duncan Kennedy, whose work in this area is the foundation of the analysis in this book.

Colleagues and students who made helpful suggestions for revisions of draft chapters include Bernadette Atuahene, Debbie Becher, Carl Bogus, Wayne Barnes, Vanessa Casado Pérez, Hanoch Dagan, Anna di Robilant, Will Feldman, Susan Fortney, Guillermo García Sanchez, Paul George, Kent Greenfield, Terri Lynn Helge, Brian Larson, Daphna Lewinsohn-Zamir, Glynn Lunney, Thomas Mitchell, Adam MacLeod, Billy Magnuson, Tim Mulvaney, Chris Odinet, Gary Orren, Carol Pauli, Andy Perlman,

Huyen Pham, Peter Reilly, Ezra Rosser, Susannah Barton Tobin, Jeff Weiss, Nancy Welsh, Jeff Willard, and Lua Kamal Yuille.

I benefited from suggestions made by participants at workshops at Roger Williams University School of Law, Texas A&M University School of Law, and the Property Works in Progress Conference at Boston University School of Law. I received insightful suggestions and reflections from students at William S. Richardson School of Law at the University of Hawai'i at Mānoa and at Texas A&M University School of Law. My thanks go to Alejandro Balandran, Carl Bergquist, Brett Bushnell, Rodney Char, Jongsok Choi, Megan Cloud, Tai Foster, Micah Hansen, Norman Hasso, Kevin Hernandez, Dustin G. Hoffman, Casey Hutnick, Britagne Johnson, Ciara Kahahane, Alexandra Lizano, Alexis Long, Toan Nguyen, Molly Parlin, Catherine Pligavko, Jason Sheffield, Jennifer Sogi, and Cheyne Tribbey.

JOSEPH WILLIAM SINGER
Cambridge, Massachusetts
5780/2020

WHAT THIS BOOK IS ABOUT

We live in a time of partisan politics where it may seem that our society has no common ground about the values that should shape our laws. The truth is that we agree about more things than most of us realize. We have common values that enable us to reason about which legal rules are just and wise. And while civil discourse may seem scarce in the political world,[1] it is the centerpiece of our court system. Lawyers have techniques to engage in civil debate about divisive issues. This book explains how persuasion from reasoned argument works, why civil discourse matters, and the tools lawyers use to argue about what the law should be.

When I told people I was writing a book on persuasion, many of them asked me how to persuade someone who is stubborn and irrational. That question gave me pause because we are—all of us—sometimes stubborn and irrational, and perhaps even for good reason. Other words for stubborn are "resolute" or "tenacious" and there is nothing wrong with holding fast to values we embrace. And research has shown that we are reluctant to change our positions even when confronted with inconvenient facts; we tend to explain those facts away to avoid cognitive dissonance. That sort of irrationality is part of human life. Nor do we come

---

1. Lilliana Mason, *Uncivil Agreement: How Politics Became Our Identity* 4 (2018) ("we are increasingly blind to our commonalities").

to our views solely on the basis of cold reason; emotion and intuition affect our evaluation of questions of justice and fairness.

At the same time, it is correct that there are preconditions to rational discourse. As the quote from Plato in the epigraph to this book acknowledges, persuasion is only possible if we are willing to take ourselves and other people seriously. Persuasion requires work, both of yourself and of others. It requires willingness to think, to question, to listen, to change. If those are lacking, then no persuasion is possible, at least not by reasoned argument. This book is not about how to talk to someone who has no interest in listening or thinking about the matter at hand. It is about those occasions when rational discourse is both possible and appropriate.

I wrote this book primarily to help law students learn how to make normative arguments about what the law should be when the legal rules are unclear or outdated. This book categorizes the arguments that lawyers use in debates about ambiguous or contested legal questions. It also explains how judges justify their decisions about what the law should be when the case involves competing values and there are plausible arguments on both sides. The goal is to provide law students a toolkit to help them engage in reasoned arguments about what the law should be.

A second audience is law professors, legal writing instructors, and clinicians who teach students how to engage in advocacy for what the law should be, as well as how to write a persuasive judicial opinion justifying why one rule is better than the alternatives.

A third audience is the general public. This book is written to be accessible to anyone who is interested in the topic of civil discourse about law and social policy. In a world where civil discourse seems scarce, we can learn something from the lawyers and judges who strive to continue to engage in it and who possess useful resources for doing so. Our political system would work better if political debates adopted some of the methods of civil discourse that lawyers have developed for use in the court system, especially the norm of showing respect for the other side and willingness to acknowledge legitimate counterarguments.

An old story has two people asking a rabbi to adjudicate their dispute. The first person makes his argument, and the rabbi says, "You're right." The second person makes his argument and the rabbi says, "You're right too." An observer objects: "But they can't both be right!" and the rabbi responds, "You're right too!"

The rabbi's last response is partly wrong and partly right. It is wrong because sometimes they both are right in the sense that competing arguments have their place in our analysis of the issue. The decision maker may conclude that both sides present compelling values, interests, and arguments and that the case is hard for exactly that reason. Conversely, the rabbi's statement is right because the case needs to be decided; someone must win and someone must lose. When we decide the case, we will need a determination that one set of arguments prevails over the other in the context at hand. This book explains the arguments we make in persuading others about what the law is or should be and the justifications we can give to choose one set of arguments over another.

Part 1 introduces the topic of civil discourse and the way lawyers use it. Chapter 1 defines civil discourse and explains how persuasion through reasoned argument works. Chapter 2 explains the techniques lawyers use in making arguments about what the law is or should be.

Part 2 identifies the most important normative arguments that lawyers use. Chapter 3 focuses on arguments that assert that someone acted wrongfully or that we should act in certain ways in relation to others, such as arguments about fairness, justice, liberty, rights, and morality. Chapter 4 focuses on arguments about the consequences of competing legal rules and the ways we seek to craft rules that promote the general welfare.

Part 3 focuses on considerations specific to the rule of law with its commitments to treating like cases alike, ensuring equal protection and due process, protecting people from unfair surprise, and recognizing when values have evolved so that legal rules need to be modernized. Chapter 5 addresses the relationships between judges and legislators in the lawmaking process in a free and democratic society and the different roles played by federal and state courts. Chapter 6 discusses the practice of creating and relying on precedent while allowing the law to change as social values and conditions evolve. Chapter 7 compares the advantages and disadvantages of rules that can be applied in a relatively mechanical fashion versus standards that can only be applied by exercising contextual judgment. Chapter 8 focuses on interpretation of ambiguous contracts, statutes, and constitutional norms.

Part 4 moves from arguments (considerations we should take into account) to justifications (reasons that we give to explain why one set of arguments should prevail over another). Chapter 9 explains framing techniques that shape background understandings, frame the question being considered, or persuade through storytelling. Chapter 10 describes how we specify what values mean in concrete cases and reconcile conflicting values by reinterpreting them, limiting their legitimate contexts, or discerning when the values do not actually conflict after all. Chapter 11 focuses on what we do when we cannot reconcile competing values by contextualizing their application to separate spheres. These methods include: balancing interests, engaging in Golden Rule or social contract reasoning, and reflecting on rules and cases to make them fit together as well as possible (reflective equilibrium).

Part 5 gives examples of normative argument in the context of three hard cases in the areas of property (Chapter 12), torts and contracts (Chapter 13), and civil rights (Chapter 14). Each chapter contains mock judicial opinions with arguments on both sides of the dispute, giving examples of how one might combine the various arguments in this book to provide justifications for alternative results.

This book includes many charts that summarize the arguments that have been presented. Those charts are collected at the end of the book in the appendix for easy reference and review.

The cover image is a photograph of the Bourne Bridge connecting Cape Cod to the mainland in Massachusetts. In the background is the Cape Cod Railroad Bridge. The two shores are within sight; they are separated, yet part of the same state. They are neighbors, not enemies. The image of the bridge suggests that it is possible to get to the other side by an act of engineering or construction. Bridges are ways to "get to the other side" in a physical world, just as persuasion offers ways to reach the other side in a debate between people. And as the image shows, there can be more than one way to get to the other side.

"But can you persuade us, if we refuse to listen to you?" said Polemarchus.

"Certainly not," replied Glaucon.

Plato, *Republic*

Don't do to others what you would not want done to you.

Hillel, *Talmud Shabbat 31a*

To be persuasive we must be believable;
to be believable we must be credible;
to be credible we must be truthful.

Edward R. Murrow

PART I.

Persuasion in a
Politically Divided Age

CHAPTER I

Why Civil Discourse Matters

§1.1 How persuasion works

If you watch television news or follow the tweeting wars, you might think that the way to argue about issues of public importance is to shout a lot, interrupt, insult your enemies, and refuse to listen to them. Well, that's one way to handle things and it may even make you feel good—for a while. But it will not achieve your goals; it will not persuade anyone to your cause. Yelling makes it harder—not easier—for others to hear you. Insults make us defensive and resistant to listening. On the other hand, when we confront injustice, we sometimes simply want to express our sense of outrage. Expressing ourselves about things that matter is often appropriate and important. But if our goal is persuasion, other tactics are needed.

How do you change someone's mind? The answer is that you cannot. Instead, you can help that person change her own mind by connecting your argument to something she already believes and values. People change their minds when they come to see their own values in a new light.[1] Persuasion ordinarily works not

---

1. Michael Austin argues that "'meaningful argument' largely entails convincing people that certain actions and beliefs are consistent with [their] core assumptions. [¶] Thus we can frame the task of political persuasion as involving the attempt to convince people to update their current beliefs with new

by convincing others to change their values, but by making them aware of values they already have that they simply had not initially thought were relevant in this situation.

The ultimate foundation of any argument is a value. Values describe interests that are central to human flourishing. They are things like privacy, dignity, liberty, equality, happiness. Values are claims about how the world should be. They are more than interests, which are things that we want or care about. Values represent our ultimate ends, things that are good in themselves. They are not merely a means to other ends; they are the things for which we want other things. They are "final" or "ultimate" ends.[2] They make life meaningful.

Arguments of justice, fairness, rights, and morality focus on explaining why people ought to act in certain ways when their conduct affects other people. Importantly, because they are claims about the way the world should be, they are things we feel entitled to demand of other people. We ask for them because we are confident that these things matter, that we have good reasons why we should act consistently with those values, and because we have not heard a good reason to act in a way that contravenes them.

Martha Nussbaum explains that "most people, when asked to generalize, make claims that are false to the complexity and the content of their actual beliefs. They need to learn what they really think."[3] For example, someone may argue that the first amendment prohibits any law that limits free speech. But does that mean that we cannot enact a law prohibiting restaurants from posting a "whites only" sign? The Constitution has been interpreted to authorize laws that regulate discriminatory speech in public accommodations to ensure equal access to the marketplace. Because we have multiple and competing values, most rules have exceptions. Because our system recognizes and protects those competing values, we make distinctions among fact situations in determining when rules should appropriately apply and when they should not apply. We may see our values in a new light when someone helps us focus on these complexities.

---

information." Michael Austin, *We Must Not Be Enemies: Restoring America's Civic Tradition* 96 (2019).

2. Henry S. Richardson, *Practical Reasoning About Final Ends* 271 (1997).
3. Martha Nussbaum, *The Fragility of Goodness* 10 (1986).

§1.2 The role of civil discourse

Civil discourse is reasoned argument about matters of public importance. We often disagree about what the law should be, and because we live in a free and democratic society, we need ways to persuade others that the legal rules we favor are both just and sensible. We cannot do that unless we have thought carefully about the issue ourselves. Nor can we persuade others unless we listen to them to understand why they see the issue differently.

Civil discourse matters because it is the way we persuade ourselves and others about who to vote for, what public policies we should support, what laws we should have, and how to interpret the laws we have. When we engage in civil discourse, we reflect on our own values and we listen to the arguments on the other side. Arguments identify things we should take into account in making a decision. Arguments often are paired with counterarguments. Considering the arguments on both sides of contested legal issues enables us to make defensible judgments and to generate reasons for our positions that express our values and that could be accepted by others. Understanding the competing values that are implicated by contested decisions may also enable us to accept reasonable compromises when we cannot come to complete agreement.

Civil discourse is not always possible. The preconditions for civil discourse are missing if the person you are talking to does not care about facts, is unwilling to listen, has no interest in seeking common ground, is willing to contradict herself without reconciling the contradiction, and is unwilling to deliberate about her own values. Civil discourse cannot occur if we lack the emotional control necessary to listen to people with whom we disagree or when there is such a power imbalance between the parties that we are not free to speak our minds. It is also impossible when someone has so much power that she does not feel the need to justify herself to others and sees no reason to do so. When you face someone like this who is also callous, cruel, or indifferent to human suffering, sometimes yelling, insulting, and mocking is all you can do.

When we think about persuasion, we usually think about persuading someone else, but the person you first have to persuade is yourself. We cannot credibly convince others that something is right or true or wise if we have not thought carefully about it. We need to reflect on our own assumptions and intuitions, and we need to be willing to learn from others. We need to be aware of our own inclination to be impatient with opposing viewpoints; we need to practice the art of listening. We should be ready to admit when we are wrong. We need to be willing to acknowledge when a hard case involves legitimate arguments on the other side. Civil discourse helps us do all these things.

§1.3 Why listening matters

Christopher McMahon teaches us that "[b]ringing a cooperative arrangement into existence will normally require some or all of the parties to make concessions."[4] Societies are cooperative arrangements, and free and democratic societies reject the authority of a particular religion or moral creed. Instead, they recognize the values of individual liberty, equality, and a democratic form of government. Ideally, government reflects the will of the people while protecting "inalienable rights" such as the equality of all persons and the freedom to "pursue happiness" in a manner compatible with the same freedoms for others. This requires us to be willing to concede some of what we might want so that we can live peacefully with others in a manner that accords others the dignity we demand for ourselves. Persuasion requires an ability to acknowledge the need for concessions. Fairness requires us to agree to appropriate concessions but not inappropriate ones.[5] The trick is knowing the difference. Only through civil discourse can we discover together what concessions are reasonable to make in a society of free and equal persons that embraces government by, for, and of the people.

The adversary system in United States courts is premised on the assumption that judges will make better and fairer decisions if they hear the strongest arguments on both sides of a hard case. If we generate those arguments, we may come to see why the case is hard. We better understand what is at stake in a decision when we focus on the pros and cons of the alternative rules of law, the multiple values implicated by the decision, and the reasons that might be given to justify a resolution one way or the other. Doing this may narrow the scope of disagreement, allow us to develop compromise solutions, preserve respect for the losing side and the losing argument, and give us some level of confidence that we are doing the right thing in a hard situation.

---

4. Christopher McMahon· *Reasonableness and Fairness: A Historical Theory* 1 (2016).
5. *Id.*

Getting to the other side means persuading others about the meaning of fairness, equality, liberty, and democracy, both in general and in particular cases. But it also means *getting* the other side—understanding them, seeing the world the way they do, learning what values they care about, what facts matter to them, and what they think those values mean for concrete cases.

I have taught several seminars at the William S. Richardson School of Law at the University of Hawai'i at Mānoa. My students pretended they were a state supreme court adjudicating a hard case that involved competing values. The first time I taught the course, a remarkable thing happened. The first student explained how she would resolve the case and gave her reasons. The second student turned to the first student and said, "Here is what I heard you saying. You think the plaintiff should win because..." and restated what the first student said. The first student responded by saying, "Yes, that's what I think." The second student then said, "Well, I agree with this, this, and this... but not that. I think the defendant should win and here is why." Then the third student spoke and did the same thing, restating both the first and second students' views and explaining what he agreed with and disagreed with.

I was stunned. Every student was able to state their opponents' position accurately, with words that those on the other side could accept. They treated the discussion as one among people who deserve respect and attention. They took the opposing arguments seriously and did not caricature or oversimplify them. Because they listened carefully, assumed the other students were acting in good faith, and tried to empathize with others, they were able to learn why someone who is trying to do the right thing might take that position. And they recognized the ways they agreed with the other students' arguments.

I was not used to hearing students at my own institution do that. They could only sometimes accurately restate an opposing position. They did not usually focus on making sure they understood other students' comments. Perhaps unintentionally, they would more often caricature another student's position, describing it selectively to show it in its worst light rather than giving it the credit it was due. They refused to acknowledge anything valid or defensible about it. They failed to see what they agreed with in other opinions and therefore missed the overlap between the opposing positions.

Persuasion is possible only if you can help someone else see their own values in a new light. When we listen, we can discover both what we disagree about and the values we have in common. By reinterpreting values, we are sometimes persuaded to change our minds.

Western classical music often changes (or modulates) from one key to another by introducing a dissonant note that does not exist in the first key but does exist in the new key. When we combine that dissonant note with notes common to both keys, we create a new chord that does not belong in the original key. Its dissonance makes us want to move to a second chord in the new key. Because the dissonant note was combined with common notes in just the right way, that second chord feels like home. What was unstable is now stable. What was moving is now at rest. A dissonant element, if combined in the right way with shared elements, can move us to another way of seeing the world. Connecting something we find hard to accept with something we already take for granted enables us to change our perspective.

The students in Hawai'i knew they could not persuade their colleagues to change their minds unless they listened carefully enough to find not only what they disagreed about but what they had in common. Showing that they heard that common note, and showing they understood the perspective animating the opposing argument, allowed them to introduce a new way of looking at their common values through a new fact or a new social context or a new analogy that the first student had not focused on.

The combination of a shared value and an unexpected element changes the significance of the shared value. That creates the possibility of persuasion. It does so because it introduces something that needs to be explained (the dissonant element) and connects it to something the other person already believes (the common element). That allows the students to come up with reasons that could be accepted by the other side and helps them view their own values in a new light.

§1.4 The importance of giving reasons

Civil discourse not only prompts careful thinking, listening, and reflection, but also requires us to put into words the reasons that exist for choosing one course of action or one legal rule over others. Reason giving helps us recognize legitimate interests and rights on both sides of a dispute and to think through appropriate resolutions of conflicting values or of competing interpretations of the same value. When we are forced to give reasons why one legal rule is fairer than another, we can more easily see and acknowledge the multiple and conflicting values that are implicated in hard cases.

Cases are hard when normative arguments that we accept as relevant tell us that there are competing values or that application of a legal norm to a case is problematic, either because there are reasons to believe it may be unfair or because it may cause social harms that outweigh any benefits. To give good reasons, we must specify the implications of abstract values, such as liberty and equality, for concrete social problems or disputes. Reasons appeal to values and they explain why proposed rules or interpretations promote or implement those values in specific fact situations. The most fundamental arguments assert reasons why we should treat each other in particular ways. We must also consider the social consequences of alternative rules. Reason giving prompts us to look for legitimate ways to justify particular rules of law to those affected by them.

When we have to justify a rule or policy to someone who objects to it by coming up with reasons they might accept, we sometimes realize that our initial view was mistaken. For twenty years, I have taught a seminar where students pretend to be the Supreme Court to discuss and decide pending cases and write opinions to explain and justify the rules of law they have chosen. Every time I teach this course, some students change their minds between their initial vote and writing the opinion. They usually do so because I ask them to articulate the strongest counterarguments raised by the other side and to respond to them. When they cannot think of a good answer to a counterargument, they may change their minds about the result.

Judges often find that an opinion "just won't write"; they cannot articulate good reasons for the result they initially settled on. Fundamentally, the object of a judicial opinion is to recite reasons for the result that could justify the result to the losing party. The idea is that anyone who thought about the matter clearly, with appropriate information and motivation, could accept this outcome as the most just way to resolve an intractable conflict involving competing values. Reason giving, if taken seriously, can change our minds.

In a free and democratic society, only public reasons can serve as appropriate justifications for public policies and laws. Public reasons are ones that could or should be accepted by people with differing perspectives, religious traditions, moral frameworks, and experiences. Persuasion in a politically divided and diverse society cannot happen if we do not recognize the different (and possibly adverse) perspectives and experiences we bring to the table when we debate issues of public importance. Our conceptions of justice may emerge from particular religious commitments or moral intuitions, but in a society of free and equal persons committed to religious liberty, we need to connect our particular moral or religious perspectives to common values. To do that we must listen to and speak to everyone— including those who oppose (or seem to oppose) our view and who look at the world differently than we do.

§1.5 Why we agree about more than we think we do

When someone convinces you to see your own values in a new light, the possibility arises for mutual understanding and agreement. We are surprised when someone has convinced us to focus on something that we care about but that we had not considered before. We are prompted to see that a value we already believe in might be a reason to change our minds. That happens when we have been made aware of something important about that value that we had not paid attention to until now.

All of us have a tendency to focus on particular aspects of a problem and particular ways of understanding our own values. If we follow the example of the students in Honolulu, and listen sympathetically to thoughtful counterarguments, we will usually realize that hard cases implicate shared values and we often agree with the values on the other side. The real dispute is often not about values but value specification.

For example, a baker who refuses to make a wedding cake for a gay couple because of his religious beliefs is a hard case because there are legitimate interests on both sides and because the values underlying those interests have competing interpretations. Both sides claim equal rights to religious freedom and property. The baker claims a right to exemption from a law when it requires him to do something that violates his religious beliefs; the customers claim a right to act in accord with their own religious beliefs without being ostracized and excluded from the marketplace open to the general public. Both sides claim property rights: one claims the right to exclude nonowners from his property while the other argues that they will not be able to acquire property on equal terms if they are excluded from the marketplace because of their religion or sexual orientation.

Both sides agree that no one can be coerced into participating in a religious ceremony. Nor can anyone declare herself exempt from following any law she dislikes simply by asserting that it violates her religion; if that were so, then laws would have no effect against people who do not want to follow them. Both sides agree, on the one hand, that there is a protected sphere of religious liberty immune from state control, but they also agree that, on the other hand, most of the time we are obligated to follow the law even if we think it is unjust or that it violates our religious beliefs. Hard cases arise when there is a plausible claim that recognition of a religious exemption from a generally valid law could be crafted that does not violate the rights of others.

None of this means that we will wind up agreeing about what to do. But it does mean that we will have a better sense of what is involved in answering the question if we pay attention both to the complexity of the issue and the fact that both sides agree on key values relevant to the decision. When the parties share common values, the real problem is how to specify what those values mean in concrete cases and the relative weight of conflicting values in different factual contexts.

Looking for shared values is critical to persuasion. If there are comparable easy cases on both sides about which everyone agrees, and if there are values that both sides accept, and if those values need specification and interpretation to apply them to a hard case, then we have a basis for discussion, mutual understanding, enlightenment, and considered argument. Persuasion can happen when we see the notes we have in common. It is harder to vilify our opponents when we see that the values they champion are ones we support as well. We may come to see why they see the issue the way they do, and they may have the chance to see things as we do.

§1.6 Seeing both sides

Given all this, the main thing to avoid in arguing about hard cases is one-sided arguments. No one will convince the baker to serve the same-sex couple if they ignore the baker's religious liberty claim or do not recognize it as a shared value. To make a plausible argument, the same-sex couple must explain how they view the value of religious liberty and what it means in specific cases. Indeed, if they focus on the baker's argument, the customers may realize that they have a religious liberty claim of their own. They can admit that religious liberty matters and then reframe the issue by asking what the right way to protect the religious liberty of both shop owners and customers is.

Rather than ignore reasonable competing arguments and the shared values championed by the other side that are actually implicated in the case, we need to explain why we interpret those values differently. We have no chance of persuading someone else without recognizing and responding to their legitimate concerns. Neither persuasion nor clear thinking is possible if we treat a hard case as if it were easy. We must also recognize when we ourselves would agree with the other person if the facts were a little different.

The good news is that persuasion by argument is possible because our values are complicated and in need of interpretation and because they often pull us in different directions. Typical arguments are often paired with typical counterarguments. For these reasons, it is easier than you might imagine to find points of overlap between your argument and the beliefs of the person you are trying to persuade. This book provides a toolkit of arguments and tips on what the most likely counterargument may be for any argument. Having this toolkit at your disposal may make it easier to build an argument that appeals to the person you are trying to persuade, even if it seems, at first glance, that you come from different worlds or value systems.

§1.7 Telling—and facing—the truth

We cannot tell the truth to the other side if we cannot face it ourselves. To persuade someone else, we must face the truth both about the argument we are making and the argument on the other side. That means that we must concede what is correct about the opposing argument and the weaknesses in our own argument. We must also distinguish between the arguments we could make and those we should make. We should not make arguments we cannot defend by reasons that an impartial judge could accept.

Of course, we do not all agree about which arguments deserve to be taken seriously. Judges themselves differ on this score. Lawyers inevitably need to make judgments about what arguments to make and which things to focus on. They also take into account the perspective of the judge they are trying to convince. At the same time, it is counterproductive to argue for a proposition that you cannot defend. Nor is it helpful to try to persuade a judge by tricking them, deflecting their attention, confusing them, or engaging their emotions so they ignore important, relevant facts. Such persuasion is not warranted, stable, or legitimate; it is unlikely to work or to last.

Beginning law students—and even many practicing lawyers—imagine that the way to win is to focus on the strong points in your argument and to ignore your weak points. That strategy can only succeed if both the lawyer on the other side and the judge are incompetent and unable to see the flaws in your reasoning. But contested cases usually bring out the strongest points on both sides. That is why it is better to acknowledge what is true in what the other side is saying and to concede when your proposed rule has some costs we would wish to avoid or when it infringes on values we seek to protect.

The only form of persuasion that is both effective and defensible is persuasion based on reasoned argument. Reasoned argument recognizes the complexity of our beliefs and values. It is generous to the other side by seeing values and intuitions we share. It does not ignore facts or distasteful consequences of the approach we favor. If a rule we are arguing for has some bad consequences, we should recognize them.

It has been said that the truth will make us free but first it will make us miserable. Here that means that warranted persuasion can occur only if we recognize the truth about the issue we are confronting and are honest about the legitimate interests and values on both sides. We should then come up with a reason why one value prevails over another when they come into conflict or why our approach is the best way to achieve everyone's legitimate interests in the long run.

If there are justifiable claims on both sides, we may not be able to decide the case without causing some unfairness. If that is so, then we should try to figure out which result would be the least unfair. If we cannot do justice without causing harm that we wish we could avoid, we should face the truth and acknowledge that harm. If a moral or legal issue is a hard one, then it is wrong—it is false both factually and morally—to pretend it is easy.

Edward R. Murrow's epigraph at the beginning of this book argues that "to be persuasive we must be believable; to be believable we must be credible; to be credible we must be truthful." He meant that we will be believed only if what we say is worthy of being believed. That can only happen if we are courageous and humble enough to recognize when we are wrong and when others are right. We must recognize what is lost as well as what is gained by any legal rule we favor. We must stand our ground when it is right to do so, and we must yield when the right is on the other side. We cannot tell the truth unless we are willing to face it ourselves.

CHAPTER 2.

How Lawyers Persuade

§2.1 Reasoned argument about common values

Lawyers know how to argue. If they are bad at it, they antagonize other people and exacerbate conflict. But if they are good at it— and good lawyers are very good at it—they know how to argue without being argumentative. They know how to persuade others not by tricks or manipulation but by finding common ground. They do so by reasoned elaboration of values we hold in common and by identifying legal rules that enable us to achieve our goals in a manner consistent with the rights of others.

Lawyers engage in moral reasoning of a special type. We do not focus on private morality—the ethics of personal and social relationships—but on public issues of law. Those legal issues involve questions about when and how the state should prohibit, regulate, or permit conduct, and about the rules governing relationships to ensure that we are treated fairly when we interact with others.

Lawyers are in a service profession—serving both our clients and the public. Lawyers work for clients and promote their interests by showing why our clients' interests serve the public interest. No one will be convinced to adopt a rule of law or public policy that helps one person unless they are confident that anyone in that person's position is entitled to similar treatment, and that the rule in question promotes the general welfare.

Good lawyers have techniques that help analyze issues and make persuasive arguments in a diverse society. When we are dealing with people that have different religious traditions, perspectives, community attachments, and values, we need something in common in order to reach accommodations that could or should be accepted by all. That requires us to build and maintain a common "civil religion" of public discourse built on common values like freedom, equality, and democracy. Lawyers have experience in doing this form of civil discourse and have developed a set of standard arguments and counterarguments that concern things we should take into account in shaping rules that promote the public interest as well as the interests of our clients.

I love music and I have an interest in playing and listening to music in my home. But what if my neighbor can hear the rock music blaring on my speakers and hates it? She has an interest in peace and quiet. What values are implicated here? What names can we give to these interests to shed light on why our competing interests matter and why they should be protected by law? A number of things comes to mind, including liberty, security, autonomy, privacy, neighborliness, freedom of expression, human flourishing, dignity, joy, happiness. In addition, we should recognize that we both want quiet enjoyment of our homes, and our rights risk jeopardizing others, so our rights have to stop somewhere to ensure that others can enjoy equal rights.

These values provide reasons for ruling one way or the other in a dispute. Values are a vocabulary for debating conflicting claims and determining what we are and are not entitled to have and to demand of others. Arguments are premised on them; they make arguments persuasive.

§2.2 The role of emotion in reasoned argument

We sometimes may think that we act either because of emotion or reason. The truth is that both affect our decision making and both are crucial to persuasion. Our emotional reaction to a situation will incline us in one direction or another; it is often key to our intuitions about who is right and who is wrong in a dispute. The first step in making a persuasive argument is to understand how the decision maker is likely to react to the situation, and that requires attention to the emotional reactions we can expect. But if emotion were the only factor in decision-making, then persuasion would hardly ever be possible; we would just stick with our initial intuitive inclinations.

Reason and argument can both take our emotional reactions into account and provide frames of reference for them. Reason giving can remind us that we have conflicting values and that there may be features of the situation we have not focused on and that need to be taken into account. Both storytelling and issue framing are so critical to persuasive argument because they can help us see the situation in a new light. Storytelling engages our sense of morality by provoking an emotional response as the narrative and characters move forward. Frames for issues can also draw attention and elicit new emotions.

We can test emotional pangs with careful reasoning and discern whether our initial intuitions are worthy of support and sufficient to justify particular outcomes. Arguments may lead us to change our minds not by making us entirely reject our initial intuitive reaction but by helping us see whether we can defend our initial intuition with credible reasons. That is only true when those reasons are worthy justifications for the result. But persuasion cannot work without emotion. When we give reasons, we do not ask others to ignore their emotions; we explain the moral significance of their emotions. Storytelling, framing the issue, and reason giving help us understand our emotional reactions, but they also put them in their proper place.

§2.3 When lawyers use arguments

Why do lawyers argue so much? Why don't they just look up the law and tell clients what the law is? Why do judges have trouble saying what the law is and why do they disagree? Part of the answer is that law comes from various sources, and these sources are often ambiguous or conflicting. Sometimes the law contains gaps that do not cover the case at hand, making it a "case of first impression." And sometimes the problem is knowing who has the right to decide a particular question. Our democratic system of government defines roles for lawmakers; for example, we distinguish between what legislatures should decide versus what judges can decide.

There are four major sources of law: (a) statutes; (b) regulations; (c) common law; and (d) constitutions. Statutes are passed by Congress or the state legislatures. Regulations are created by administrative agencies to provide specific guidance on what statutes mean. Common law rules are crafted by state judges when they decide civil suits involving people who were injured by others, suffered a breach of contract, or have a dispute about property rights. Constitutions structure our governmental institutions and define fundamental rights that cannot be taken away by statute or common law.

People sue each other in court to vindicate their rights against others as they understand them under the law. Because all these sources of law are ambiguous and even conflicting, lawyers for both sides make arguments about what the law is. In doing that, they inevitably also argue about what the law should be.

§2.4 How lawyers argue

§2.4.1 STORYTELLING

Human beings love stories. They are a crucial means by which we make sense of the world and they are one of the ways we engage in moral reflection and reasoning. Stories are how we characterize and understand people and events. I moved to Cambridge, Massachusetts after graduating college. Did I do that (a) to attend graduate school; (b) to be near my twin brother; (c) to begin my adult life; (d) to make my parents proud; or (e) to do what I could to repair the world? The way we describe events and persons frames our perception of who they are and why their acts matter. And the sequence of events in a story identifies a hero, a problem, adversaries (or even villains), and potential solutions.

Consider a condominium owner who places an American flag on his balcony the day after 9/11. The country has been attacked by foreign enemies and we have suffered grievous and heartbreaking losses. Public servants have lost their lives trying to save the wounded. The flag is a show of solidarity, patriotism, and defiance.

This is a good story. But here is a different version.

The condominium association has rules that prohibit any decorations on the balconies, including flags, wind chimes, and political posters. Those rules protect the property rights of all the owners, and they all agreed to abide by them when they bought their units. Ensuring a uniform, clean appearance for the building creates a serene and peaceful environment, avoids disputes among owners, and protects the market value of the property. If one owner has a legal right to fly the American flag, then others can post signs as well, including offensive ones. Owners are free to express their patriotism, but they are not free to ignore the promises they made when they moved in, and they are not free to violate the property rights of their neighbors.

Which story is the right way to understand the situation? The answer to that question matters. The way you tell the story can shape how you understand the values at stake, the reasonable expectations of the actors, and the legitimacy of alternative outcomes.

Some years ago, I had trouble explaining to students why there were property law issues when companies close factories. The students did not see what I saw, and the only way I found to explain what I was thinking was to tell a story. Here is what happened.

When the U.S. Steel Company closed a factory in Youngstown, Ohio, the union tried to keep the workers' jobs by offering to buy the factory from the employer so the employees could continue operating the factory. When the company refused, the workers sued to compel the company to sell the factory to the workers at its fair market value. The company argued that it had the right to do what it liked with its own property.

The workers argued that the factory was being closed not because it was unprofitable, but because the company could make greater profits elsewhere. If the workers bought the factory, they could protect the company's property rights by a money payment that would allow it to invest elsewhere to generate those higher profits. After all, the company was going to fire the workers and sell the property to someone; the buyer might as well be the workers. Since the workers cared more about having jobs in their own community, they could continue to operate the factory profitably, supporting the local economy, while protecting the interests of both sides. The workers also argued that the company had made oral statements over the years that led the workers to rely on the continued existence of the factory in the community as long as it was profitable. Closing the factory violated expectations they had based both on a longstanding course of conduct and on informal assurances.

The company won the lawsuit. The court held that it was free to do what it wanted with the factory. Rather than sell it to the workers at fair market value, the company demolished it.[1]

When I taught this case to my first-year property students, back in the 1980s, they thought the court was right. More than that, they thought the

---

1. Local 1330, *United Steel Workers v. United States Steel Corp.*, 631 F.2d 1264 (6th Cir. 1980); Joseph William Singer, *The Reliance Interest in Property*, 40 Stan. L. Rev. 611 (1988).

case was easy. I was teaching property, after all, and, under the law, the company owns the factory and the workers do not own their jobs. Nor did the company make any explicit promises to the workers that the factory would remain open—assurances yes, but no promises, no contract. So we have no contract and no property rights. The workers lose. To my students, the workers' arguments were frivolous.

I had wanted the students to understand why the workers brought the case and why there were arguments based on established contract and property law principles that could have justified ruling in the workers' favor. But I was unable to persuade them that the case was harder than it might appear.

So I thought to myself: when had the students, in their own lives, ever relied on informal representations or based their expectations on the prior conduct of others? That led me to tell the students the following story. Imagine, I said, that your professors here at the law school decided that students were not working hard enough and that those at the bottom of the class would not be good lawyers. To solve this problem, we professors decided to change our grading policy. Look to the left of you; look to the right of you. One of you will not be here in the fall. We have decided to flunk the bottom third of the class at the end of the semester. Good luck on your exams! Do you have any legal rights?

The students knew this was just a hypothetical scenario and that it had not happened. But they were outraged. More than that, they were certain that, if the school did this, it would be illegal.

"You can't change the rules like that in the middle of the game," they said. "If we had known you were going to do that, we would have gone to another law school."

"What rules?" I asked. "We have no written rules that say we cannot change our grading system. Where did we make that promise?"

"The catalog," they answered. (Today it would be the school website.)

"Where does it say that in the catalog?" I asked. "I've read it and all the school's promotional material. There is no promise like that of any kind. And look here, on the first page of the catalog. It says: 'everything in this catalog is subject to change without notice.' That means that even if we had made a promise, we are free to change the rules at any time. Didn't you read that part?"

The students started arguing about customs in the law school market, the prior behavior of the school, norms of appropriate conduct in higher education, and, ultimately, about the unfairness of changing rules in the middle of the game.

"That's all well and good," I said, "but we are managers of property owned by a charitable entity. It has empowered us to run the school. It owns the school and can do what it likes with its own property, can't it? If you wanted assurances that we would not change grading practices in the middle of your time here at the law school, why didn't you bargain for protection from changes in policy like that?"

That story made the workers' argument comprehensible to the students. It did so for two reasons. First, the students could empathize with the workers because the students could see how they themselves might be in the same position and might want protection in that situation. Second, the story helped them see how the workers' claims connected with values they themselves held. By asking them to play a role, to reason by analogy, and to see how they were implicated in the workers' story, the students learned something about themselves and their own values. That enabled them to connect their own experience to those of workers facing a plant closing, to empathize with them, and to see why someone might think an injustice had occurred.

I'm not claiming I changed anyone's mind. But the story did help them see how the workers understood their situation. And it helped the students see that their own sense of fairness might justify greater sympathy with the workers than they had initially thought. That understanding led them to see why the worker's legal claim might be not frivolous after all.

§2.4.2 FRAMING THE QUESTION

Law professor and judge Robert Keeton said that he could win any argument if he got to frame the question. Framing the question is one way to get others to understand the values implicated in a hard case and to see the story in a way that helps us identify the villain and the victim.

Consider a case in which a shopping center owner sold the neighboring property with a deed that included the paved area next to the shopping center. That was a mistake; the owner never meant to sell that paved area. Moreover, the buyers did not think they were buying that area. It was evident to any observer that delivery trucks needed that area to deliver goods to the back of the stores. Only after buying the neighboring land did the buyer hire a surveyor and discover that the deed given to the buyer by the seller included that paved area.

Should the courts reform the deed to make it consistent with the parties' mutual understanding at the time of the sale, either by moving the border or by letting the shopping center owner continue to use the paved area for its deliveries? Or should the courts place the border between the properties at the line indicated in the deed, forcing the seller to negotiate with the buyer to try to buy that strip of land back or tear down part of its building to create an adequate delivery route?

The buyer may frame the question this way: should a real estate buyer be able to rely on the written terms in the deed? If that answer is yes, then why should the seller be allowed to take back property that it has sold? Shouldn't you be careful in writing the deed to make sure it reflects the property you want to sell? Each of these questions suggests that the buyer should win.

The seller may frame the question this way: when the parties to a contract make a mutual mistake, and the contract terms do not reflect their understanding of their deal, should the courts enforce the deal that both parties agree they intended to make or should the courts allow one of the parties to get more than they bargained and paid for merely because of a mistake in formalizing their arrangement? Why should the buyer get something they did not pay for? Would the buyer be making the same argument if the mistake had gone the other way and the shopping center was claiming half the parcel the buyer thought they had just bought? These questions suggests the seller should win.

Framing the question is a way to shape our understanding of the moral conflict in ways that enable us to empathize with the party making the claim and to understand the reasons why they should prevail. It is also a way of telling the story and placing blame.

§2.4.3 INTERPRETING VALUES

Values are meaningful but contested. Most Americans support the values of liberty, equality, and democracy, and we have a general sense of what those values mean. But we do not agree on the role those values play in specific cases. Values need to be interpreted and they require specification to determine how to apply them in concrete instances. Sometimes persuasion occurs by drawing someone's attention to a particular case that engages a basic value in a different way than they may have appreciated.

For example, do zoning laws protect property rights or infringe on them? The answer depends on whether we are focusing on the freedom to use what we own or security from having our property harmed by what others do with their property. Consider a zoning law that requires an owner to leave half of her land free from construction to preserve open space between homes and to ensure proper drainage and prevent flash floods. A conservative person who opposes "big government" may see the law as an oppressive restriction on property rights, depriving the owner of the freedom to do what she wants with her own property. But many conservatives who want "small government" actually support zoning laws. They do so because zoning laws protect property rights. If you want to own a house in a neighborhood free from factories, the only way to accomplish that is for the legal system to limit what can be done on land owned by your neighbors.

The abstract value of "private property" hides within it competing interpretations and values. Once we understand that, we realize that we need to specify which of the competing values should prevail when they come into conflict.

Similarly, a political liberal may be a strong advocate of freedom of speech. She may be delighted to see a house painted in rainbow colors to indicate support for gay rights and might oppose a zoning law that limits the colors you can use when you paint your house. But that same person will be opposed to allowing a neighbor to burn a cross on her own property because that symbol tells Jews and African Americans that they are not welcome in the neighborhood and that they may even be in danger. The Fair Housing Act prohibits such acts of intimidation because they prevent people from acquiring property because of their race or religion.[2] Does free speech mean that one can say what one likes, no matter what that is, or can speech be limited to protect equal access to the marketplace and to ensure security in one's home?

When we apply abstract values to concrete cases, we not only find out that they hide within themselves competing conceptions of what those values mean, we may find that those values are limited by other values. If we focus on fact situations that involve value conflicts, we can more easily

---

2. 42 U.S.C. §3617.

recognize those complexities. We can then understand the need to make choices about what our values really are when they apply to the real world. When we specify what values mean in concrete instances, we reduce abstract norms to formulations we can apply in practice to contested cases.

§2.4.4 LEARNING NEW FACTS

Sometimes we see our own values in a new light when we learn new facts. Consider that for most of U.S. history, people viewed swamps as undesirable and tried to eliminate them. You cannot plant most crops or easily build anything in a swamp. But then environmental scientists found out why swamps—renamed as wetlands—are important to ecology. They discovered why filling in wetlands might harm the environment, cause pollution, destroy helpful wildlife, and make property nearby unstable and vulnerable. That led to environmental statutes that preserve wetlands. New facts changed minds.

In upholding the right of a state to criminalize same-sex sexual relationships, Justice Lewis Powell apparently commented that he had never met a gay person, not knowing that one of his clerks was gay.[3] Would it have made a difference to Justice Powell if he had been aware of how many people are gay? Would it have mattered to him to know that some of the people he knew and cared about were gay? Maybe. When large numbers of gay people began to come out and acknowledge their sexual orientation to friends and family, that new information placed the issue in a different light, and it seems that it did change many people's attitudes.

§2.4.5 EVALUATING CONSEQUENCES

One way to resolve a dispute is to apply an existing rule, regardless of its consequences. If the rule is a good one, why ignore it just because the facts here are a little different than before? That approach, however, is inconsistent with the pragmatic approach to conflict resolution typical of American law. Our traditions teach us to care about the consequences of enforcing rules to those affected by them.

If someone argues that a rule is a good one because it has certain good

---

3. Adam Liptak, *Exhibit A for a Major Shift: Justices' Gay Clerks*, N.Y. Times, June 8, 2013.

consequences, the opposing side may argue that the rule is a bad one because of its bad consequences. The decision maker must determine what the consequences of the rule are likely to be, including whether the parties are right to claim that the rule will have the consequences they claim it will have. She will then have to decide if the good consequences outweigh the bad or vice versa and whether any other rule would make us better off than the proposed rule.

For example, consider a statutory rule that allows someone to choose who will get ownership of his house when he dies by writing a formal will witnessed by two people. This rule protects freedom and dignity by allowing us to dispose of our own property after death and it (often) protects our family members. But that rule should not apply if a man leaves his house to his grandson in his will and the grandson murders the grandfather to prevent the grandfather from changing his mind.[4] Applying the rule of free disposition to benefit a murderer contravenes the likely intent of the grandfather and the legislature that wrote the wills statute. It rewards someone for an evil act. A rule that lets you write a will to transfer your property at death should not—and will not—be extended to a situation where someone abuses that trust by murder.

Rules must be interpreted to determine their legitimate scope of application. They may be narrowed if they lead to unforeseen negative consequences or if they contravene competing values that violate the reasons why we created the rule in the first place. Americans have traditionally taken a pragmatic approach to law. We do not apply rules of law mechanically, regardless of their consequences. We care about the facts, the situation surrounding the dispute, the competing values that may not have been fully considered when the rule was initially created. We are not smart enough to predict all the things that might happen in the future. We are not smart enough to create rules that will be fair regardless of the circumstances. We shape rules over time, as we learn new things and as we confront situations we had not previously thought about.

§2.4.6 JUSTIFICATIONS

Justifications are different from arguments, as I use those words in this book. An argument is a claim that we should take into account. When there

---

4. Riggs v. Palmer, 115 N.Y. 506 (1889).

are legitimate arguments on both sides, we need a reason to believe that one argument should prevail over the other. That reason, or set of reasons, is what I mean by a justification.

Suppose my neighbor has solar panels on her house and complains that my trees have grown so tall that they block the sun and hamper her ability to get benefit from her investment. She asks me to cut my trees down or at least prune them so they don't extend above the second story of her house. She wants to save money and protect the environment and claims a right to enjoy the benefits of her efforts to do these things.

On the other hand, I like my trees. Part of the reason I bought my house is because it was surrounded by trees that remind me of the forest behind my childhood home. I like the shade they provide; I like the rustle of leaves in the wind; I like the vivid colors in the fall. They are my trees and I want to keep them as tall as they are. I have a right to plant trees in my own yard and enjoy them when they grow.

My neighbor and I both have good arguments. But each argument, stated by itself, is one-sided. I claim a right to use my property as I see fit; she claims a right to be secure from harm. We need a way to recognize the legitimate arguments on both sides and then to give a justification for why one argument prevails over the other in this fact situation. Such a justification would recognize that owners have rights to plant trees and to install solar panels. When those rights clash, we need a reason to pick one right over the other. We might conclude that protecting the planet should take precedence over mere aesthetic concerns. We might conclude, to the contrary, that owners are free to install solar panels but that right does not allow them to stop neighbors from similarly using their property as they see fit. A justification acknowledges the interests and rights on both sides and tries to give reasons why the line should be drawn here rather than there.

Justifications differ from arguments because they recognize the existence of counterarguments and they go on to give reasons why one argument should be accepted in a particular context over another argument. Justifications may also explain why presented arguments are plausible or unreasonable. They may concede that both sides have good arguments to support their proposed rules and then explain why one rule should prevail in this context. They may contextualize social situations to explain when an interest should be protected and when it should not be protected. The goal of a justification is to give reasons that could or should be accepted by the losing side and that could be seen as reasonable for a society of free and equal persons.

To prevent awkwardness, I will sometimes use the general term "argument" to refer both to claims each side makes and to justifications that explain why one claim should prevail over another. Lawyers use the general term "argument" to describe both. I introduce the separate term "justification" to emphasize that an argument cannot be persuasive unless it acknowledges the legitimate claims on both sides and provides reasons why one set of arguments should prevail over the other. In other words, persuasive arguments provide justifications for adopting one set of arguments over another.

A prime example of a justification is the Golden Rule. All formulations of the Golden Rule help generate solutions that could be accepted by all persons. Some version of the Golden Rule is at the heart of a lot of moral reasoning and imagination because it is based on the notion that every person matters. One version of the Golden Rule focuses on affirmatively treating others as you would want to be treated; another version focuses on refraining from actions you would not want others to do to you. Either way, a key method to evaluate a social or legal practice is to imagine whether you would be happy if you were on the other side. That was part of the point of asking students to imagine their reaction if a law school told them it had decided to flunk one-third of them. Rules of law are fair only if they apply both to us and to others. Thinking about whether we would feel fairly treated if a rule of law applied to us—or to those we love—is one of the most powerful ways to see our own values in a new light.

Given the fact that people are different and want different things, the "platinum rule" tells us: do not do unto others what they would not want done to themselves. The focus here is not on treating others as we would want to be treated but on understanding how they want to be treated; assuming what they want is legitimate, we can treat them with dignity by showing them the same deference we would like them to show us. Seeing a problem or situation from someone else's perspective helps us to imagine alternative ways of framing questions and may change our perception about what facts matter. Doing this may affect the way we understand and balance competing interests. It tempers self-interest by enabling us to recognize the interests of other people. And it offers a recognizable way to justify a choice in a hard case.

§2.4.7 RULES & PRINCIPLES

When judges resolve conflicts, they do not just announce who won. Rather, they identify a general principle that will apply in the future to similar cases. The principle may be in the form of a rigid rule (18-year-olds can vote) or a flexible standard (don't drive negligently). The goal of arguments and justifications is to craft appropriate principles to guide judges in the future and to let people know what they are and are not allowed to do. That means that arguments are persuasive only if they identify a general principle that could be adopted to handle this case—and cases like it—in the future.

§2.5 Procedural tools

§2.5.1 BURDENS OF PROOF

This book focuses on normative arguments, but a crucial device that lawyers and judges use to shape debate about contested issues of law is to allocate burdens of proof. One way that judges manage the uncertainties of the legal system is by deciding which person has the burden of convincing the decision maker about the issue. In civil lawsuits, the burden is usually on the plaintiff (the one bringing the lawsuit) to show that the defendant (the one the lawsuit is brought against) engaged in wrongful actions and that those actions violated the plaintiff's legal rights. The law defines both the plaintiff's rights and the defendant's obligations. At the same time, the law may identify defenses to the claim.

For example, the plaintiff may allege that the defendant struck him. If so, that constitutes the tort[5] of battery and the plaintiff may be entitled to damages because of it. But if the defendant acted in self-defense, then no tort was committed. The defendant is likely to have the burden of proving that he acted in self-defense.

Several issues arise here. First, how convinced does the jury have to be that the claim has been proven? In a criminal trial, we require the jury to be convinced beyond a reasonable doubt. However, in a civil case brought by one person against another, the burden is much lower. The plaintiff need only prove the wrong by a preponderance of the evidence. That means that it is more likely than not that the claim has been proven. If the jury cannot

---

5. Tort law provides civil remedies when someone was injured by the wrongdoing of another.

figure out what happened and thinks the chances are 50-50 that the plaintiff is correct, then the plaintiff will lose. The plaintiff will win if the jury thinks that the chance the plaintiff is correct is more likely than the chance that the defendant is correct. Some civil rights need to be proven by clear and convincing evidence—a standard that is closer to the criminal law standard of "beyond a reasonable doubt." Lawyers will argue about what the standard should be in civil cases; how convinced must the fact finder be that the plaintiff's rights were violated?

Second, what things does the plaintiff have to prove and what things does the defendant have to prove? Suppose the plaintiff can easily prove that the defendant hit the plaintiff, but it is not clear whether the defendant acted in self-defense. If the defendant has the burden of proving the defendant acted in self-defense and cannot prove that by a preponderance of the evidence, the plaintiff will win. But if the plaintiff has the burden of proving the defendant did not act in self-defense—and cannot prove that by the preponderance of the evidence—the defendant will win. Changing the burden of proof may affect the outcome of the case.

§2.5.2 NEGOTIATION

There are many ways we can legitimately persuade others—and our-selves—about which rule of law should govern conduct or a human rela-tionship. Lawyers' main focus is on convincing a judge about what the law should be or on getting legislators to agree to enact a statute. However, per-suasion also occurs in the context of negotiations between private parties, either to settle a lawsuit or to negotiate a business deal. Negotiation among persons differs from persuading a judge or legislator. It is helpful to know a few important features of negotiation.[6]

When two or more parties are negotiating to achieve a mutually bene-ficial outcome, the goal is to fashion an arrangement that the parties will accept because they are better off with the agreement than without it. Three concepts are helpful in understanding negotiation: (1) the distinction be-tween positions and interests; (2) identifying the parties' best alternatives

---

6. Helpful introductions to negotiation include Roger Fisher, William L. Ury &Bruce Patton, *Getting to Yes: Negotiating Agreement Without Giving In* (3d ed. rev. ed. 2011); Robert H. Mnookin, *Beyond Winning: Negotiating to Create Value in Deals and Disputes* (2000). *See also* Robert H. Mnookin, *Bargaining with the Devil: When to Negotiate, When to Fight* (2010).

to a negotiated agreement (BATNA); and (3) adopting a problem-solving approach.

(1) INTERESTS VERSUS POSITIONS. When people begin negotiations, they may start by stating their position, i.e., what they want or ask for. What happens if the initial positions conflict and the parties stubbornly cling to them? In that case, no agreement is possible. Suppose, for example, that a prospective employee wants the freedom to leave a job and work for another employer but the prospective employer will only offer the job if the employee signs a noncompete agreement promising not to work for a competitor for two years after leaving the job. The positions conflict—either the employee will or will not be restrained from working for a competitor.

If we focus on why the parties are making these demands, we may be able to identify their underlying interests. The employee, for example, may be worried about earning a living for that two-year period when she is not able to seek or accept a job in the same field. The employer may be worried about the employee stealing trade secrets or sharing them with the new employer.

Each party is demanding one thing because they think it is the best or only way to get another thing. If the parties communicate and work together, changing their focus from their initial positions to their underlying interests, they may be able to find out why the other side is asking for something. It may become evident that they can achieve their ultimate goal in an alternative way. They may reach a mutually beneficial agreement that satisfies those underlying interests without acquiescing to the initial demands.

(2) BEST ALTERNATIVE TO A NEGOTIATED AGREEMENT (BATNA). Slamming your fist on the table and demanding that someone else capitulate and accept your demands will be completely ineffective if that person has other ways of satisfying her interests so that she can walk away without a deal with you. She will only agree to the deal you propose if it is better than her alternatives. When you negotiate, you must estimate what her likely alternatives are, and create an option that is better than those alternatives. The same goes for you. Only when the parties can craft an option that is better than their best alternatives can a deal happen.

(3) DEVELOP A PROBLEM-SOLVING PROCESS. You are more likely to understand the other side's interests and offer them something that is better

than their alternatives if you get to know them well enough to figure out what they want and need. You can do that if you think about the negotiation as working together to solve a joint problem. When you do that, you can develop a process for interacting that can unearth each side's real goals and develop alternative ways of achieving them. That requires a process that enables the parties to trust each other enough to listen and to reveal what they really want.

§2.6 Bad lawyering

Persuasion is justified and works well when it adheres to norms of honesty, humility, and respect. Good lawyers do this very well. That is not to say that persuasive techniques cannot be misused. Here is a short (incomplete) list of what not to do:

- ☑ Do not lie or state things that are not true.
- ☑ Do not mislead or state half-truths or lie by omission. When your proposed rule causes unavoidable harm, admit it while explaining why the good your approach achieves justifies the rule despite its bad consequences.
- ☑ Do not misrepresent your opponent's argument, argue against a "straw man" (an argument your opponent does not really hold) or a "red herring" (an argument that is not relevant to the question to be decided).
- ☑ Do not create a false dichotomy by suggesting that only two options are available when that is not true.
- ☑ Do not try to persuade by deflecting attention from important facts and values.
- ☑ Do not cite legal precedents that support your position while failing to identify and discuss those that undermine your position.
- ☑ Do not ignore legitimate interests and rights on the other side.
- ☑ Do not use insults as a way to disparage the opposing position. Ridiculing the other side does not demonstrate strength but insecurity.

PART 2.

Normative Arguments

CHAPTER 3.

Rights, Fairness, Justice, Morality

§3.1 Interests & values

Philosophers and theologians have argued for thousands of years about the ultimate foundation for claims that actions or states of affairs are right or wrong, just or unjust. Some may find these values embedded in the word of God, others in human nature or our ability to reason, and still others in our original or evolving traditions, customs, written constitutions, laws, or precedents. Luckily, we do not need to engage deeply with these metaethical discussions; nor do we need to identify a single, ultimate, and incontrovertible foundation for claims of justice and fairness. It is enough to accept the fact that human beings have a sense of morality—and it is a good thing that we do.[1]

Human beings judge behavior and human interests by reference to what Charles Taylor calls "strong evaluations."[2] We have a sense of justice. We do not just accept the world as it is; we have convictions about how it ought to be and how we should treat others. Rather than debate whether we should avoid wronging

---

1. Susan Neiman, *Moral Clarity: A Guide for Grown-Up Idealists* (rev. ed. 2009); Jedediah Purdy, *For Common Things: Irony, Trust, and Commitment in America Today* (1999).

2. Charles Taylor, 1 *Human Agency and Language: Philosophical Papers* 66 (1985).

others or treating others unfairly, we are better off spending our time identifying the values we do hold, the moral intuitions we have, and our sense of what those mean in concrete fact situations. When we make claims of rights, fairness, justice, or morality, we may be asserting that some states of affairs are unjust, such as a highly unequal distribution of income, and that laws need to be passed to prevent or repair those inequities. Shared values, intuitions, and commitments can serve as contextually basic foundations for normative argument.[3]

The Declaration of Independence expresses this insight by asserting that some values are "self-evident." We start from shared values and commitments we embrace, along with our settled intuitions, and reason from those. We are a society that values freedom, equality, and democracy. We do not question or abandon those values. They are the framework we use to evaluate everything else.

One way to specify what these values mean in the context of concrete, real-world problems is to identify interests that each side has in a dispute and then convert those interests into values. We have desires but we also evaluate those desires to see if they are things we should desire. I like having friends over to my house for dinner; I have an interest in doing so. I have a right to invite guests to my home because I am entitled to freedom of association, autonomy, and a meaningful life, and those things include having friends. Calling an interest a value means that it is a final end—something that is good in itself rather than something that enables us to achieve something else.

Arguments based on rights, fairness, justice, and morality focus both on the obligations we have toward others and the rights we have against them. Philosophers may characterize these arguments as deontological because they describe moral duties toward others. They may also be based on social contract theory that imagines what political and legal structures and rules we would adopt if we were creating a society of free and equal persons from scratch and seeking universal consent to the laws we were creating. They may be based on a conception of what makes human life meaningful and how the good or virtuous person should act. Or they may be based on the

---

3. Mark Timmons, *Morality Without Foundations: A Defense of Ethical Contextualism* (1999).

idea that we have an obligation to give reasons for the ways our actions affect others.[4]

§3.2 A hypo:[5] firecrackers

Consider this case: The Commonwealth of Massachusetts bans the sale of fireworks for personal use. Only licensed professionals are allowed to buy and use them. The state treats fireworks as ultrahazardous products because they are dangerous and easy to misuse. Even though their sale and use are banned in Massachusetts, they are easily available next door in New Hampshire, in stores not far from the border.

> Lawful sale of fireworks in New Hampshire that injure a child in Massachusetts where they are banned

Every year there are a certain number of injuries to children in Massachusetts from fireworks used by nonprofessionals. Assume a Massachusetts father goes to New Hampshire to buy some firecrackers and brings them illegally back to his home. He gives some to his minor child who uses them with his friend from next door. One of the firecrackers misfires and hits the friend, blinding him. The parents of the injured boy sue the New Hampshire store for selling an item banned in Massachusetts to someone who foreseeably took it back to his home in Massachusetts where it caused grievous harm to a child.

Assume that Massachusetts law imposes strict liability on the seller of a dangerous and illegal product for any harms that it may cause, while New Hampshire immunizes the store from liability on the grounds that the product is safe if used properly and that the culpable actor is the father who negligently entrusted the firecrackers to his minor son with inadequate supervision.

This hypo presents a conflict of laws problem: should the law of Massachusetts or New Hampshire apply when a product legally sold in New

---

4. Proponents of these forms of reasoning include philosophers like Aristotle, John Locke, Immanuel Kant, John Rawls, Margaret Urban Walker, Christine Korsgaard, T.M. Scanlon, Michael Sandel, Susan Muller Okin, and Jennifer Nedelsky.

5. For those not familiar with the lingo used in law school classes, a "hypo" is a hypothetical (or a real) situation that focuses discussion about what legal rule should regulate the parties' actions and their relationship. In a hypo like this, sometimes facts are made up to highlight or sharpen the value conflicts implicated in the choice between alternative legal rules.

Hampshire causes injury in Massachusetts and when the place of injury imposes liability on the seller for the harm? It may help also to know that the traditional rule of law applied to conflicts of law of this type is that the law of the place of injury applies unless that is fundamentally unfair to the defendant.

The main types of "rights" arguments we will consider are:

- rights of freedom of action versus rights of security
- legitimate versus wrongful conduct
- individualism or self-reliance versus altruism
- reasonable expectations
- fairness, dignity, & equality
- distributive justice
- liberty, reasonableness, & human flourishing

§3.3 Rights arguments

§3.3.1 RIGHTS OF FREEDOM OF ACTION VERSUS RIGHTS OF SECURITY

Rights arguments are claims that one is entitled to do something (a claim of freedom of action) or to be protected from some type of harm caused by another's actions (a claim of security). These claims are often summarized by saying that one has a "right" to engage in an action or to be protected from someone else's conduct. Arguments of this kind rest on assertions about justice and fairness in social relationships.

In a classic work of legal scholarship, Wesley Hohfeld noted that what he called "rights" or "claims" are associated with correlative "duties" on others.[6] If I have a right to exclude nonowners from my house, they have a duty not to enter my house without my permission. Rights of this kind are defined by the scope and content of the duties they place on others. Confusingly, we typically use the word "right" to refer both to a right of freedom of action (a liberty interest where one has no duty not to act in that way) and a right

Claims place duties on others.

Liberties may make others vulnerable to harm.

---

6. Wesley Hohfeld, *Some Fundamental Legal Conceptions as Applied in Judicial Reasoning*, 23 Yale L.J. 16 (1913).

of security (which imposes duties on others). We are secure to the extent that others have duties not to harm us or our interests.

Conversely, "liberty" or "privilege" claims promote freedom of action. They define acts I am free to do or have no duty not to do; others have no right to stop me from doing those things. Just as rights correlate with duties on others, liberties (or freedoms) are associated with correlative vulnerabilities on others who may be affected by my actions. If I am free to build and operate a gas station across the street from your gas station, you are vulnerable to losing profits, or even going out of business, because my business will compete with yours. Businesses are therefore vulnerable because they have no right to be protected from ordinary competition.

In our firecracker hypo, the injured child will argue that he has a right to security. The law of his home state bans the sale of firecrackers because the lawmakers believe they are too dangerous to be used by nonprofessionals. He has a right to bodily integrity and safety. He cannot enjoy that right unless businesses have a duty not to sell dangerous products like firecrackers to the general public or, if they do sell them, to compensate victims for resulting harms that they would not have suffered if the products had not been made available to the public. While the store may be free to sell firecrackers in New Hampshire, that right ends when the store sells them to a Massachusetts resident who is likely to bring them back to his home state, where they cause injury. Massachusetts residents have a right to be protected from actions across the border that foreseeably cause injury to them at home.

On the other side, the store will claim a right of freedom of action. The law of its home state gives it the right to open a fireworks business and to sell firecrackers. It has a right to look to the law of the place where it operates to engage in business. While it is true that firecrackers can be dangerous, they also can be used safely. It is not possible to ensure that firecrackers never harm people, but the New Hampshire legislature considers them safe enough for general use. While it is true that this makes the public vulnerable to harm that would not exist if the products were banned, people have an interest in using firecrackers for recreation and are capable, if they are careful, of using them safely. The law cannot make people completely safe while ensuring our freedom. We could, for example, substantially reduce highway deaths by making and enforcing a 25 mph speed limit. Lawmakers have determined that freedom to drive faster than that is worth the vulnerability to harm that higher speed limits cause. We tolerate a fair amount of vulnerability in order to enjoy freedom of action.

A claim that one has a right is usually an evaluative assertion that another person has wrongfully harmed another and that we have duties not to engage in those harmful actions. A claim that one should be free to act without liability or limitation by government is an evaluative assertion that human liberty or autonomy requires the right to engage in the protected activity even if it affects or harms others.

§3.3.2 LEGITIMATE VERSUS WRONGFUL CONDUCT

Moral claims directly assert the rightness or wrongness of actions. Because we are talking about human relationships and disputes about claims of harm, one side will argue that they did nothing wrong while the other side will argue that the other side did commit a wrong that caused harm.

The injured boy claims that the store acted wrongfully when it intentionally sold a dangerous product knowing it was likely to cause serious harm to children, and knowing the Massachusetts buyer was likely to bring it illegally back to his home state. According to the Massachusetts legislature, firecrackers are similar to prohibited substances like heroin or highly dangerous and regulated items like explosives. Selling firecrackers to a Massachusetts resident, knowing they are illegal in Massachusetts and that many such buyers bring them illegally back home, is equivalent to wildly firing a gun across state borders not caring if it hits anyone on the other side. The boy has a right to be protected against wrongful conduct like this.

Moral claims are about right and wrong behavior

Conversely, the New Hampshire legislature believes that the risks are small compared to the benefits and so selling firecrackers is not wrongful. The store has a right to operate in New Hampshire according to New Hampshire law. If anyone did anything blameworthy here, according to both the store and the New Hampshire legislature, it was the father who wrongly entrusted the firecrackers to his son without adequate supervision. The store would argue that it did nothing wrong by selling a product that is legal in New Hampshire. It acted legitimately and is not to blame for the boy's injury.

§3.3.3 INDIVIDUALISM & SELF-RELIANCE V. ALTRUISM

In determining whether an act is wrongful, we often look to moral frameworks that fluctuate between obligations to look out for the well-being of others and rights to pursue happiness in whatever ways best suit us. We cannot pursue happiness if we need to think about how each of our actions affects every other person in the world, but we also cannot pursue happiness if we are not secure from harm. We all have a moral duty to rely on ourselves; we cannot ask others to do everything for us. At the same time, it is wrong not to avoid serious harm to others when we can do so at little cost to ourselves, and it is often wrong to engage in conduct that poses a foreseeable risk of harm to others.

> Individualism and self-reliance: look out for yourself
>
> Altruism: look out for others

A claim that we should be free to pursue our goals at will embraces the morality of individualism (the freedom to do what we think best for ourselves) and self-reliance (each person is responsible for looking out for herself). A claim that we have an obligation to look out for others to ensure that our actions do not wrongfully harm them embraces the morality of altruism (attention to the needs and desires of other people as well as our own). No one embraces either of these moral frameworks exclusively; we combine them, although we may not all do so in the same way.

The injured boy will claim that the store has a duty to look out for his interests as well as its own and to refrain from actions that are likely to cause harm to others. He will argue that harms caused by firecrackers are well known, as is the fact that their sale and possession are illegal in Massachusetts, and that a buyer from that state is likely to bring them unlawfully back to his home. The store therefore has an obligation to compensate the victim when the store has breached its duties to protect him.

Conversely, the store will argue that it is the parents' obligation to look out for their own son's welfare, and therefore the parents are responsible along with his friend's father who failed to adequately supervise his son's use of the firecrackers. The store is entitled to sell firecrackers in a state that allows them to be possessed and used, and it has no duty to assume that Massachusetts buyers will break the law by bringing them back home for use in a state where they are illegal. New Hampshire law allows stores to sell firecrackers without regard to their potential negative effects on others.

The store bears no responsibility or moral liability for the harms that its product may cause.

§3.3.4 REASONABLE EXPECTATIONS

Human beings are planners. When we act to achieve ends we have chosen, we rely on knowing beforehand certain facts about the world. We have expectations about what our actions will accomplish, whom they will benefit or harm, how other people are likely to act, and what the rules in force tell us about whether our actions are lawful. We rely on others; we foresee the effects of our actions; we object when others subject us to unfair surprise. All these arguments relate to judgments about what we can or should reasonably expect to happen when we choose our ends and act to achieve them, as well as our expectations about how other people will and should act.

What do we expect?

Are those expectations reasonable?

What do we have a right to expect?

Did someone rely on a law or the actions of others?

Was that reliance reasonable?

Would liability unfairly surprise the store?

Was the harm foreseeable?

The injured boy will argue that he has the right to rely on the protection of his home state's law. The store cannot reasonably expect that a Massachusetts customer might not bring the firecrackers back to Massachusetts because it is common knowledge that this is a frequent occurrence. Nor is it reasonable for the store to rely on the protection of its home state law or hide behind it when it sells its products to residents of a neighboring state and they foreseeably cause injury there.

The store will argue that it reasonably relied on the law of New Hampshire applying to its sale and its store located there. It would be unfairly surprised by application of another state's law when it did no business there. Nor could it foresee that its customer would break the law and illegally bring the firecrackers back home in violation of Massachusetts law. Many nonresidents have friends in New Hampshire and the customer could well have been planning to use the firecrackers lawfully in the place of sale. Nor should the store be required to treat its customers like criminals and refuse to sell products on the chance that they will misuse those products or use them in a way that violates the law. The store will argue that it has the right to rely on its customers using its products carefully and legally. It cannot foresee which buyers will misuse its fireworks and it would unfairly surprise the store to make it responsible for the conduct of its customers when the law of the place where it operates immunizes it from such liability.

§3.3.5 FAIRNESS, DIGNITY & EQUALITY

Fairness concerns just relationships. Each of us has a right to be treated with dignity. That means that we must treat other people as beings of utmost worth; human beings matter. We are valuable and we are irreplaceable. Treating other people fairly means giving them their due and respecting their claim to freedom and dignity and to humane and equal treatment.

Fairness

Human dignity

Equal rights

The injured boy will argue that it is unfair for the store to make money from selling dangerous products that unreasonably and foreseeably cause serious harm to children. Even if the store has some claim that it has a right to be free to engage in lawful business in its home state and to rely on local laws that immunize it from liability, it cannot hide behind those laws when it sells goods to residents of the neighboring state. If you cannot confine your conduct, or the consequences of your conduct, to the state that immunizes you, then you lose any right to the protection of your own state's law and you are fairly governed by the laws of the state that holds you responsible for the harm you foreseeably caused there. The store cannot legitimately close its eyes to the harms it is doing to children across the border. The injured boy has an equal right to the protection of his home state's laws and an equal right to the liberty of being safe from foreseeable harm caused by actions his state lawmakers have criminalized because it views them as unreasonably dangerous.

The store will argue that it has not treated the boy unfairly or denied him equal dignity. No one is questioning the fact that the customer broke Massachusetts law by bringing the firecrackers illegally back to his home state. While the Massachusetts legislature deems the seller morally culpable for the harm to the child, New Hampshire lawmakers disagree. According to New Hampshire, fault, if any, lies with the father of the child that used the firecrackers in a way that injured the child's friend. There are many ways parents can protect their children from harms of this kind. Massachusetts also has alternative ways to protect its children. Massachusetts could, for example, increase enforcement of its fireworks laws or impose harsher penalties for violating them. By New Hampshire standards, the store is not the cause of the harm. It is not morally responsible for the actions of its customers in bringing fireworks illegally into the boy's home state.

The boy may claim the right to protection of his home state's law, but the store has an equal right to the protection of the only place where it does business. It is unfair to subject the store to Massachusetts law by imposing that law extraterritorially on acts that take place in other states where they are lawful. It is also unfair to make the store pay for what its lawmakers view as an accident, and not its fault. Not every tragedy has a legal remedy.

§3.3.6 DISTRIBUTIVE JUSTICE

Distributive justice issues concern the fair allocation of property as well as the fair distribution of the benefits and burdens of social life and economic activity. While social welfare arguments tend to focus on the way rules benefit society as a whole by promoting the general welfare, distributive arguments focus on the distribution of those benefits and of the burdens needed to generate the benefits.

Legal scholars who do economic analysis of law tend to divide all issues into those of efficiency (increasing the size of the economic pie) and distribution (determining who gets slices of that pie and how big they are). Reducing issues to these two categories may suggest that issues of fairness can be reduced to questions of quantity and measured in dollar amounts. But arguments about distributive fairness cannot be reduced to discussions about dollars; if we had to choose between being injured and compensated for the injury versus never being injured at all, it is clear what we would choose. Money often cannot "make us whole." Nonetheless, distributive issues of wealth, resources, rights, or vulnerabilities are a way to argue normatively about the fairness of legal rules.

Distributive justice as the fair allocation of the benefits and burdens of social life

The injured boy will argue, for example, that people cannot live or flourish if they are not safe from harm. Even if a determination was made by the New Hampshire legislature that the benefits of making fireworks available to the general public outweigh the costs, that does not mean that those who are injured by private fireworks use should bear the resulting economic burdens. The boy will argue that the store should bear the burden of paying for the harms it causes when it sells unreasonably dangerous products to people likely to bring them illegally to a state that bans them. Between the innocent child and the store that made a living by selling attractive but dangerous products likely to end up in a state that bans them, the store should pay for the damages. Under Massachusetts legal standards, the store has money in the bank that rightly belongs to the victims of its conduct, and Massachusetts law should take precedence if the store's conduct spills over into Massachusetts and causes harm there.

The store will argue, in contrast, that since it is not morally responsible for the accident under New Hampshire law, forcing it to pay for damages outside Massachusetts makes it an unwitting insurer of all its customers and their friends when they leave New Hampshire. It is not fair for the store to bear this financial burden. If the state where the boy lives wants to ensure compensation for victims of injuries, it can do so through a social security program or a universal health insurance system or placing liability on the father who acted negligently inside Massachusetts. It is wrong for the state to impose that burden on a private actor from out of state who did not act negligently and did not directly cause the harm, at least according to the standards of its home state. Even if Massachusetts views the store as having acted wrongfully, that does not mean that the store should bear monetary responsibility for the resulting harms. People have a duty to look out for themselves and their children by responsible behavior and the person who should pay the healthcare costs is the parent of the injured boy's friend rather than the store.

§3.3.7 LIBERTY, REASONABLENESS & HUMAN FLOURISHING

Paradoxically, the concept of liberty is used both to support "deregulation" and "regulation." One version of liberty focuses on rights of freedom of action: we should be free to choose our own ends, to live our own lives, to make our own mistakes. Some versions of this argument focus on the idea of deregulation, meaning removing legal constraints on free action. The Declaration of Independence asserts that we have the right to pursue happiness. That does not mean that we are interested only in pleasure; it means that we are entitled to arrangements that enable human beings to flourish. Human flourishing is not possible unless we have social, economic, political, and legal infrastructures that make it possible for us to exercise autonomy.

An alternative conception of liberty recognizes that we are only free if we are safe and secure. Liberty means freedom of action, but we cannot have freedom of action unless we are also secure from harm. My liberty to move my fist ends at your face (unless I am acting in self-defense). If I am worried about being shot by strangers every time I leave my house, I will be discouraged from doing so. Philosophers like Thomas Hobbes and John Locke teach us that the first reason for government is to protect us from injury inflicted by other people. They argued that we created government so we could have the laws that regulate social interaction to enable us to live our lives fully by being safe from harm and enjoying legal and economic institutions and rules that promote our well-being. Knowing that there is a state with a police force and courts to enforce criminal law makes me feel safer than I would be in a place that had no law and no law enforcement at all. At the same time, if I am afraid that the police will see me as a criminal because of my appearance or dress or the color of my skin, that also will discourage me from leaving my home and prevent me from enjoying the benefits of freedom of movement; such fears inhibit my liberty. Liberty can be enhanced by having laws and regulations that ensure that those laws are administered in a fair and equal manner and that promote a reasonable compromise between freedom of action and security.

Human beings can pursue happiness and flourish only if we are both free to live our own lives on our own terms and if we have obligations to act so that others have the same opportunity. The law uses normative arguments and reasoning to determine when my free actions end and your security begins. It is obvious that we could not live if we never focused on achieving our own interests and needs, but we also must acknowledge that we cannot ignore the effects our actions have on others. The legal system expresses this dilemma—and this goal—in terms of reasonableness. We ask what a reasonable person would do in this situation or what law creates the right framework for enabling us to enjoy liberty compatible with like liberty for others.

The injured boy will argue that his liberty interests are at stake if a store can locate right across the border and unreasonably act in violation of the laws of his home state by selling dangerous products it knows are almost certain to cause injury in the boy's home state. The boy's liberty has been violated by the store's actions. While New Hampshire defines liberty as the freedom to sell, possess, and use fireworks, Massachusetts defines liberty as freedom from harm caused by fireworks. Therefore, while New Hampshire does not consider the store liable for the child's blindness, Massachusetts does, and the boy has as much right as the store does to liberty. If your conduct foreseeably causes injury in a state whose laws are intended to protect its people from harm, you cannot complain if those laws apply to you. You are not entitled to the liberties of action granted by your home state if you cannot confine your conduct, or the reasonably foreseeable consequences of your conduct, to the immunizing state.

The store will argue that its liberty interests are implicated if it has no right to the immunity from liability granted by the state in which it does business. It is unreasonable to subject it to liability because a third party brings its products illegally to another state. While the child victim has a strong right to security, his security was endangered by his friend's father, not the store. Massachusetts has the right to regulate the conduct of stores within its borders, but it does not have the legitimate power to regulate the liberty of stores located in another state, no matter how close that state is.

SUMMARY OF RIGHTS ARGUMENTS

RIGHTS, FAIRNESS, JUSTICE

Interests & Values

- What interests does each person have?
- What values are served by protecting those interests?
- Why should those interests be protected and who has a duty to protect them?

Rights

Freedom of action	Security

Morality

Legitimate conduct	Wrongful conduct
Individualism	Altruism

Reasonable Expectations

- Did someone rely on actions or representations of another?
  - Was that reliance reasonable?
- Was the harm reasonably foreseeable?
- Would liability subject anyone to unfair surprise?

Fairness & Equality

- Is the action or rule fair to both parties?
- Does it treat each person with dignity?
- Does it treat each person with equal concern and respect?

Distributive Justice

- Does the rule create a fair distribution of the benefits and burdens of social life?
- Does a rule create an undue or disproportionate burden?

Liberty & Human Flourishing

- Does the rule promote liberty, meaning the right accommodation of freedom and security?
- Is the rule reasonable? Does it promote appropriate concessions among free and equal persons?
- Does the rule enable each human being to flourish?

CHAPTER 4

Consequences, Social Welfare, Costs & Benefits

§4.1 Social welfare

"We the People of the United States, in Order to form a more perfect Union, establish Justice, insure domestic Tranquility, provide for the common defense, promote the general Welfare, and secure the Blessings of Liberty to ourselves and our Posterity, do ordain and establish this Constitution for the United States of America." So begins the U.S. Constitution. The Constitution's goal was to make life better for everyone.[1] Some of those ends focus on justice and liberty; those values describe behavior or states of affairs that are right or wrong. Other goals of the Constitution are to promote "tranquility," "the common defense," and "general welfare." These goals are as important as liberty and justice and they suggest a different way of thinking about the reasons we can offer to justify legal rules or public policies.

Social welfare arguments concern efforts to adopt rules that have the best overall outcomes for society as a whole. Rights and

---

1. Of course, at the time the Constitution was written and adopted, "everyone" clearly did not include enslaved persons; nor did it necessarily extend to women of any race or to people who did not own property. The discussion here focuses on what we mean (or should mean) today when we talk about promoting the "general welfare."

fairness arguments make moral judgments about behavior directly, distinguishing conduct that is wrongful from conduct that is legitimate. In contrast, social welfare arguments make moral judgments indirectly; they first try to identify the consequences of competing rules, then evaluate those consequences to identify the good and the bad consequences, and finally compare the good and bad consequences to choose rules that make us as a society better off. While rights arguments tend to focus on individual conduct and to make a judgment about whether it is wrongful, social welfare arguments focus on the social effects of alternative rules to determine the best outcomes for society as a whole.

Consequences of legal rules or public policies

Bad consequences are "costs"

Good consequences are "benefits"

Compare the costs and benefits of competing rules to pick the rule that best promotes social welfare

Social welfare is defined by an ultimate goal, such as happiness, pleasure, human flourishing, welfare, well-being, or wealth.

Social welfare arguments have two steps. First, we consider the actual effects of various legal rules by figuring out what will (or is likely to) happen in the world if we adopt one rule rather than another. How will the facts of the world change with different rules? What incentives do the rules create and how will they affect human choices about how to behave? We focus on the ways the rules will affect behavior and what the consequences of that behavior will be. This is why social welfare arguments are a form of consequentialism. Consequentialist reasoning judges rules based on their consequences.

The second stage of social welfare reasoning incorporates moral judgment. We evaluate the effects of alternative rules as good or bad by reference to some ultimate goal. Adopting rules that promote happiness by focusing on their consequences was the basis of the utilitarian approach to moral reasoning and it has been an important feature of normative arguments about the law. Utilitarian moral theories ask us to consider the ways that legal rules promote an end such as happiness, utility,[2] pleasure, human flourishing, welfare, well-being, or wealth. Rules that promote these things are benefits; rules that detract from them are costs. Once we have classified the effects as benefits or costs to society, then we compare the costs and

---

2. Philosophers have used the concept of "utility" to mean happiness or welfare or well-being.

benefits of alternative rules to help us adopt a rule that promotes social welfare better than any alternative rules we are considering.

For this analysis to work, we must identify the ultimate end so that we can evaluate the consequences of rules by a common metric, such as happiness or welfare. Lawyers sometimes use economic analysis to provide that metric; they measure costs and benefits in dollar terms and compare them to see whether a rule promotes or undermines social wealth or welfare. But lawyers may also analyze costs and benefits in a qualitative rather than a quantitative manner, balancing competing interests to see what rules make us better off, all things considered.

It is important to understand that a rational analysis requires consideration of the net consequences of alternative rules. That is because almost all rules have both good and bad consequences. We must consider the costs and benefits of one rule and compare them to the costs and benefits of another rule. An argument that criticizes a rule because it imposes costs on some people is not an argument at all. Most rules impose both costs and benefits. The fact that a rule has costs does not tell us that its costs are greater than its benefits. What we are interested in are net costs and benefits. We look at both the costs and the benefits of any rule to figure out whether, on balance, its benefits outweigh its costs or vice versa. And a rule that imposes greater costs than benefits may still be the preferred option if the only alternative is a rule that has even higher net costs (where costs also outweigh benefits).

Some versions of consequentialism or utilitarianism try to eschew moral judgment by asking us to take human preferences as they are (not as we think they should be) and then ask how the rules affect preference satisfaction, rather than utility, welfare, or human flourishing. While expressed preferences are a useful criterion to consider, utilitarian philosophers generally do not measure social welfare by reference to preferences without some amount of judgment about those preferences. For example, in determining whether society is better off if we prohibit assault and battery, we do not add into the equation the pleasure that sadists get from beating up other people. That preference is illegitimate, at least in a society governed by our society's fundamental values and commitments to human rights. Perhaps another society, such as a militaristic one, might validate and honor cruelty and count the desire to be cruel as something to add into the equation. Our society does not do that. Utilitarian philosophers recommend morally constrained utilitarianism, where we consider and add into the analysis preferences that are not inconsistent with our fundamental political values, such as liberty, equality, and justice.[3]

Some scholars argue that we should never judge preferences because people have a right to decide what is good for them. Letting each person determine what is best for themselves arguably promotes autonomy. Autonomy is a general moral concept that is at the base of much of our thinking about justice and liberty. My own view, and that of most consequentialist philosophers, is that "satisfaction of preferences, whatever they happen to be" is an interpretation of the concept of autonomy that is not defensible in a society committed to individual rights. Preferences that are geared to effects on others, and which deny the rights and liberty of others, should not count in any calculus of costs and benefits of legal rules. For that reason, preference-based theories need to be supplemented by recognition that the value of autonomy requires ignoring (not valuing) unjust preferences.

The idea of counting each person's preferences, whatever they may be, and counting them equally, and adding up to see how it comes out, is supposedly based on the concept of equality. Pure preference-based theories are problematic because they endanger social justice. If we count preferences, whatever they are, and add them up, without any moral filter at all, then the resulting set of rules could justify oppression. For example, if a majority wants to establish their religion as the official state religion and to suppress dissenters, and if each person's preferences are counted equally, the cost-benefit analysis may find that society is "better off" by repressing minority religions. The preference-based method for promoting equality needs a moral filtering device so that basic equality rights are protected before the adding process happens. We cannot treat people equally by just adding preferences; some policies and laws are off the table, because they do not meet minimum standards of fairness and justice in a free and democratic society that is committed to the idea that each person has an equal right to pursue happiness.

All this means that when we assess the social value of the costs and benefits of any rule, we should take into account the relevant consequences. Preferences or effects that are illegitimate are not part of a valid cost-benefit calculus in a society that respects individual rights.

---

3. *See* Mark Timmons, Moral Theory 267–270 (2002).

§4.2 Common social welfare arguments

§4.2.1 INCENTIVES

One focus of social welfare arguments is the incentives created by legal rules. How will people behave in response to differing rules, given the motivations and interests that people have, and will that conduct be beneficial or harmful to society as a whole? Is it behavior we want to encourage or discourage?

The boy in our firecracker hypo will argue that society is better off by banning the private use of firecrackers by nonprofessionals. One way to give stores an incentive to refrain from selling firecrackers to nonprofessionals is to make those stores financially liable for any harms caused by the products they sell. Such liability will increase the costs of doing business by making the products more expensive. That, in turn, will discourage consumers from buying them, decreasing sales to Massachusetts residents and lowering the risk of harm inside Massachusetts.

> What incentives do rules create?
> How will people respond to rules?
> How will they behave?
> Will their behavior be harmful or beneficial to society?
> Should it be encouraged or discouraged?

The store will argue in response that, unlike Massachusetts, New Hampshire wants to give stores incentives to make fireworks available to customers. Fireworks make people happy and they are safe enough for consumer use. Immunizing businesses from liability for any harms caused by their products lowers business costs and makes the product less expensive and more attractive to customers. While it is true that fireworks cause injuries, we can avoid those injuries in other ways by giving customers incentives to use fireworks safely, perhaps through better instructions.

§4.2.2 PROMOTION OF INVESTMENT

Social welfare improves if businesses invest in socially beneficial goods and services. That prompts us to ask: which legal rule will better promote socially desirable investment that generates benefits greater than its costs? Conversely, we want to discourage investment in things that cause more harm than good. Investment arguments are a subset of arguments about incentives. The focus here is to adopt incentives that promote desirable economic investment which, in turn, provides jobs, profits, useful economic activity, wealth, and welfare.

The boy will argue that Massachusetts has correctly determined that the harms of fireworks use outweigh any benefits. Criminalization and the imposition of liability will helpfully discourage the manufacture and sale of these socially harmful products. This is not an industry in which we want to promote investment—quite the opposite. Deterring investment in consumer fireworks is the best way to promote social welfare.

The store will argue that the New Hampshire rule promotes desirable economic investment in products that people want and which cause more good than harm. Banning consumers from buying fireworks or making the store liable for any accidents arising from use of its products will discourage socially desirable investment with attendant loss of jobs, economic activity, and pleasure. While there are significant costs associated with the sale of firecrackers, those costs can be mitigated in other ways. Protecting the store from liability will promote desirable investment.

Promote investment in
economic activity

As long as it promotes
social welfare

§4.2.3 COST INTERNALIZATION

Making a business pay for the harms it causes arguably makes the business internalize the costs that it imposes on society. If a business cannot pay both the costs of making the product and the costs of compensating those injured by the product, then it is possible that the product causes more harm than good and should be banned. Cost-internalization arguments seek to make businesses account for the social costs of their products.

The boy will argue that the store is making money because its profits exceeds its costs, but that is only true because the store is not being made to pay for the social costs of its activity. If the store is immune from liability, its profit-loss calculations may be positive, but if it had to compensate the dozens of people injured by its products every year, things might look different. If people are rendered blind, or lose their hands, their choices about how to live have been limited. Their costs have also risen because injured people need medical care, rehabilitation, training on how to live with their new physical condition. And because Massachusetts views the sale of fireworks as harmful, those victims have suffered a wrong that needs redress from the standpoint of justice. We provide victims of wrongful conduct the right to civil recourse by bringing the wrongdoers into court to account for their conduct and to partially make up for it by payment of damages.[4] The store obviously pays for the costs of manufacture, purchase, and distribution of its goods but if it does not also have to pay for the costs its goods impose on others, it may have a positive profit-loss comparison when it is really causing more harm than good. If it were forced to internalize the external consequences (costs) of its conduct, it may find the social costs of its activity exceed its private benefits. If that is so, then its behavior may well be socially harmful and should be discouraged. If it cannot make a profit when it is forced to compensate its external victims, then it arguably causes more harm than good and should go out of business.

When should we be required to internalize the external costs of our activities by paying for the harms we cause?

Will liability help us determine whether our actions cause more good than harm?

The store will note that the cost-internalization argument can go both ways. By using the fireworks in an unsafe manner and demanding compensation from the store, the user is trying to externalize the costs of enjoying the fireworks onto the store. Why not internalize those costs by better supervising your children or buying accident insurance? Deciding which party should internalize the external costs of its activity requires a moral judgment about who is morally responsible for the harm—but that is exactly what the two states disagree about. While Massachusetts lawmakers find the store morally blameworthy, New Hampshire does not. Liquor stores are not (usually) liable if people drink and drive; the morally responsible person is the drunk driver. The store should not have to internalize costs that it did not create and is not morally responsible for. Those who use fireworks should internalize the costs of their own activity by being careful or by buying insurance; they should not shift the costs of their own activity onto others.

---

4. John C.P. Goldberg & Benjamin C. Zipursky, *Civil Recourse Defended: A Reply to Posner, Calabresi, Rustad, Chamallas, and Robinette*, 88 Ind. L. J. 569 (2013); Benjamin C. Zipursky & John C.P. Goldberg, *Torts as Wrongs*, 88 Tex. L. Rev. 917 (2010).

§4.2.4 COST-BENEFIT ANALYSIS

Cost-benefit analysis compares the costs and benefits of a rule that imposes liability on the store and with the costs and benefits of a rule that immunizes the store from liability. So far, we have focused on arguments that focus on particular aspects of cost-benefit analysis and that may comprise parts of an argument focused on promoting social welfare.

When we ask what incentives a rule creates, we are trying to figure out how people will respond to the rule; what conduct will the rule encourage or discourage? That is a necessary step to figure out what the consequences of the rule may be. When we focus on investment promotion, we are assuming that a major goal of legal rules is to promote economic activity so that people have jobs and wealth and security while discouraging socially harmful conduct. When we focus on cost internalization, we are considering whether we can promote the general welfare by choosing rules that shape conduct by making actors consider the consequences of their actions for other people.

All these arguments are part of a larger strategy that considers the likely consequences of alternative rules, evaluates those consequences as desirable or undesirable, tries to assess the magnitude of those effects, and then compares the benefits and the harms of the alternative rules. The goal of these arguments is to help us compare the costs and benefits of alternative rules so we can choose the rule that leads to the better outcome for us all. Remember that this requires comparing the costs and benefits of one possible rule with the costs and benefits of a different rule.

The boy will argue that the Massachusetts legislature determined that the costs of private fireworks use outweigh its benefits so they should be banned. Because they are illegal and ultrahazardous products, anyone who provides them to another has engaged in a wrongful act and should be financially responsible for resulting harms. Financial responsibility will discourage the creation and distribution of fireworks and may be a necessary addition to criminal law. Because many people use fireworks safely, it is extremely hard to prevent their use entirely. Despite the ban, they are used commonly in Massachusetts.[5] There are limits to the ability of criminal law to prevent the use of fireworks. The police cannot be everywhere, and people do not like to "tell on their neighbors." If the goal is to ban or discourage

---

5. I see and hear them used by neighbors every summer in Massachusetts...

their private use (because their costs exceed their benefits), imposing financial liability on the seller is a useful way to help achieve that goal because it may discourage sales and decrease the costs imposed on society by private fireworks use.

Compare the costs and benefits of alternative rules to see whether they benefit or harm society

The store will argue that Massachusetts is free to make that judgment for Massachusetts stores, but it cannot legitimately externalize that judgment onto a store operating legally in New Hamp-

If they both benefit society, which rule benefits society the most?

shire where a different judgment has been made about the relative costs and benefits of fireworks. Massachusetts has every right to impose liability on Massachusetts actors, but it does not have the right to regulate what happens in another state just because of the unilateral act of a customer illegally bringing fireworks back to Massachusetts.

When two states come to different judgments about the relative costs and benefits of a legal rule, they should consider the costs and benefits of imposing their law on other states. The boy may argue that it is legitimate for Massachusetts to impose its law on a New Hampshire store because New Hampshire has no right to grant its stores immunity if their conduct spills over to Massachusetts and has consequences there. Massachusetts has a right to force New Hampshire stores to internalize the external costs of their conduct on the people of Massachusetts. Even if New Hampshire would benefit from immunizing its stores for the harms they cause, the costs of that policy in Massachusetts outweigh those benefits.

In response, the store will argue that the vast majority of states agree with New Hampshire. While Massachusetts is free to adopt a minority policy for its stores and its people, it has no right to externalize its laws onto actors operating lawfully in other states. Applying its law to conduct in New Hampshire in an extraterritorial manner interferes with New Hampshire sovereignty, preventing its residents from passing their own laws and being governed by them. Massachusetts has no right to externalize the costs of its own laws onto New Hampshire citizens who are following New Hampshire law. Even if Massachusetts would derive some benefit from imposing liability on a New Hampshire store, those benefits are lower than the costs of preventing New Hampshire from managing its own economic activity within its borders.

Resolving this dispute over sovereignty requires recognizing that each state is seeking to impose its policy on the other and each party is asking the other party to internalize the external costs of its conduct. The boy will argue that allowing New Hampshire to promote conduct that blinds children in Massachusetts would make all of us worse off. On balance, immunity rules should be confined to the states that adopt them; everyone is better off if states are free to apply their laws to protect their people from harm. The store will argue, in contrast, that we are all better off if states refrain from regulating conduct in other states unless that conduct intentionally causes harm over the border (such as firing a gun across the border and intentionally injuring or killing someone).

§4.3 Efficiency analysis

§4.3.1 TRANSACTION COSTS

Some legal scholars have created a way to argue about the overall consequences of alternative legal rules by using economic analysis. This is a rich field of inquiry and this discussion can only scratch the surface. Economists assign dollar values to costs and benefits so that they can be easily compared. When we are choosing between two different possible legal rules, we add the costs and benefits of each rule to see whether they would make society better off or worse off. If one makes us better off and the other makes us worse off, it is easy to know what to do. If they both make us better off, we choose the one that promotes the best overall outcome. Choosing the rule that promotes the best social outcome is said to promote economic efficiency.

Economists often make a number of simplifying assumptions. First, they generally assume that all effects of a rule can be converted to dollar amounts. Second, they figure out what makes people better off by asking what they prefer and gleaning that from their behavior or revealed preferences, perhaps ignoring preferences that violate basic human rights. Third, they take for granted the existing distribution of wealth and human capabilities.

Fourth, economists assume that we are generally better off if we are free to solve our own problems without government interference. For example, someone who objects to the activity of another can offer to pay the other person to stop engaging in what would otherwise be lawful activity. Conversely, one could compensate someone else for the harms caused by one's own conduct in order to get them to agree to allow that activity to continue.

The legal system should intervene only if there are reasons that people cannot solve their problems on their own and the government can do better.

This leads to a crucial question: are there impediments to bargaining that prevent people from entering private transactions to achieve results that promote their welfare and the welfare of others affected by their actions? The answer is "yes." Deals do not happen automatically; it takes time and effort to bargain with others. It requires a willingness to compromise, a process for getting to know the other person and perhaps generate trust, legal and technical assistance, and the effort of figuring out what the other person wants. Impediments to agreement like these are called transaction costs, and they may be substantial.

On the other hand, the costs of choosing and passing laws or allowing courts to adjudicate private disputes are also substantial. Those administrative costs may be bigger than or smaller than transaction costs. Economists think it makes sense to ask which way of solving the problem is cheapest, easiest, and most likely to generate results that promote efficiency: private bargaining or lawsuits?

Ronald Coase's article, *The Problem of Social Cost*,[6] started this form of argument by criticizing the idea that we can promote welfare by making actors internalize the external or social costs of their activity. He noted that internalization arguments make moral judgments about which activities should be discouraged. But when there are reasonable arguments on both sides, he thought that moral or justice arguments provide no solution because they are exactly what we are arguing about. He suggested instead that we focus on asking whether private transactions could achieve socially desirable results or whether, on the contrary, those deals will not happen because the costs of transacting are too high, in which case adopting legal rules to achieve the social-welfare-maximizing result might be appropriate if the costs of law enforcement are lower than the costs of private transactions.

For example, the idea that the New Hampshire fireworks seller should internalize the costs of its business activities on Massachusetts residents assumes that the business is causing harms which should be discouraged. Coase argued, in contrast, that the problem arises because the two states have different views on whether the activity is wrongful. If we want the

---

6. 3 J. L. & Econ 1. (1960).

seller to internalize the external costs of its activities on Massachusetts victims, we could just as easily ask Massachusetts residents to compensate the seller for the loss of its lawful business in New Hampshire.

Coase argued that problems arise when activities conflict, and if both activities are lawful and desired, we cannot say (without making a contested moral claim) which actor should appropriately internalize its external costs. The problem involves joint costs that the parties are imposing on each other. Rather than make a moral judgment about which party should bear the costs of their interaction, Coase argued that we should look at the costs and benefits of alternative rules and figure out the legal rule that does the best job of promoting social welfare.[7]

Coase emphasized that parties are free to bargain around property rights and rules of law. Just because the law assigns an entitlement to one party, that does not mean it will stay there. I own my house so you cannot enter without my consent, but if you offer me enough to induce me to sell, that can be changed, giving you ownership rights to the house. Liability rules are similar. For example, a recreational facility in New Hampshire may provide a space where people can set off fireworks. If the law places liability on the facility for any accidents that happen there, it may ask its guests to sign a contract waiving the right to sue the facility for any injuries that happen on its property. Conversely, if the law immunizes the facility from liability for any injuries that occur from using fireworks on its property, guests may bargain for agreements that make the facility pay if the guests suffer injury while at the facility.

Consider a case where a resort hotel in Florida builds an addition to its facility that places a shadow over the beach of the neighboring hotel for most of the day.[8] Assume also that this harm could have been avoided by building the addition in a place that did not create a shadow on either parcel. The law in almost all states allows the addition to be built without liability; each owner is free to build as they like on their own land, as long as they comply with relevant zoning and environmental laws. But the fact that it is lawful to construct the addition and impose an avoidable shadow

---

7. Recall that cost-benefit analysis, done well, will not eschew moral judgments. When conduct violates widely shared values, we appropriately do not add in the benefits of that activity in a reasonable cost-benefit calculus.

8. Fontainebleau Hotel v. Forty-Five Twenty-Five, Inc., 114 So. 2d 357 (Fla. Dist. Ct. App. 1959).

on the neighbor does not necessarily mean that is what will happen. The neighbor could avoid the construction—and the resulting harm—by offering the builder compensation not to build or inducing the builder to relocate the addition elsewhere.

Assume the addition would raise the market value of the hotel where it is built by $10 million and cost the neighbor $6 million by reducing the market value of the neighbor's property by that amount. If we simplify the problem and ignore other costs and benefits, that means that social wealth will be higher if the addition is built: the benefit is $4 million more than the cost so construction increases the wealth of the two parties.

What would happen if the builder is free to build without liability for the harm caused by the shadow on the neighbor, as current law generally allows? The answer is that the builder will go ahead. The neighbor will not pay more than $6 million to avoid a loss of $6 million and the builder will not accept anything less than $10 million to forgo a $10 million gain. Any offer by the neighbor would be rejected by the builder and the addition will be built.

What happens if we reverse the rules? Suppose the law gave the neighbor the right to stop the construction. The builder might try to offer the neighbor enough money to induce the neighbor to allow the construction to happen by waiving the neighbor's legal right to stop it from happening. But because the construction imposes a $6 million cost on the neighbor, the neighbor will agree to the construction only if the builder offers it more than that amount. Since the construction will provide benefits to the builder of $10 million, the parties may be able to negotiate for an amount between $6 and $10 million which will make both of them better off than if they had no agreement at all. If, for example, the builder offered the neighbor $8 million to get the neighbor to agree to allow the construction, and the neighbor cares only about profit maximization, the neighbor might agree to the deal. It would suffer a $6 million loss from the construction but be compensated for it by an $8 million payment; it would be better off by $2 million. The builder will be paying $8 million to induce the neighbor to waive its right to stop the construction but that would be worth it since the builder will garner a $10 million gain. In that scenario, if they reach a deal, each party is better off by $2 million.

If we assume that the costs of transacting are zero, the construction will happen whether the law gives the builder a right to build without liability or the law makes the builder liable for the external costs of the project on the neighbor. If there are zero transaction costs, the choice between the two legal rules has no effect on the outcome; the "efficient" or socially desirable result will happen no matter what the rule is. Under one rule, the legal entitlements will remain the same; under the other, one party will buy the other's entitlement. Either rule we adopt has the same outcome.

The distribution of the benefits and burdens of the project will of course be very different under the two different rules. If the builder is free to build without liability, the neighbor suffers a $6 million loss and the builder has a $10 million gain; if the neighbor has the right to be protected from the avoidable shadow, the parties will share the $4 million surplus (the difference between the joint benefits and joint costs of the project). They might each get half of the $4 million or it could be distributed some other way, depending on how the negotiations go.

We have been assuming that there are no transaction costs. But there are always transaction costs. When there are transaction costs, then the choice of legal rule may affect efficiency, or the ability of the rules to promote social welfare. If the numbers we are using are correct, the project would benefit society (the benefits outweigh the costs by $4 million) and should go forward. That happy result will occur if there is no liability on the builder. The builder will not relinquish its right to build since the neighbor will not offer more money to stop the deal than the builder will make by going forward with it.

Are there barriers to transacting that might prevent people from solving their problems by contract?

If the law assigns an entitlement to a person, how likely is it that others will contract with that person to get her to transfer or waive her rights?

However, the building project may not go forward if the neighbor is given the legal right to stop it. If the builder is liable for the costs its project imposes on the neighbor, the parties will have to negotiate to reach an agreement where the neighbor waives its right to stop the construction. If the costs of arranging that deal are substantial, they may prevent the social-welfare-maximizing result from occurring.

Each side also has imperfect information about the price at which the other side would be willing to agree to a deal. The neighbor may ask for more than $10 million; even if the builder explains that that will cause the builder to lose money on the deal, the neighbor may not believe that representation. After all, they are bargaining, and each is trying to get the most it can out of the deal. The bargaining process may also generate hard feelings; after all, the builder is asking for the right to harm the neighbor's business and even violate its property rights. The bargaining process may break down or be prolonged; legal fees may escalate, and time may pass, making alternative investments relatively more attractive. If the process of bargaining breaks down, the costs of transacting may prevent a result that an impartial observer with perfect information would have thought was beneficial to society.

Lawmakers may determine that, on balance, construction of hotel additions is beneficial to society even if they affect the profits of neighboring hotels by imposing shadows on them. Adopting a rule of no liability will therefore, in general, promote this socially beneficial result while imposing liability may inhibit projects that benefit the community. If that is true, then lawmakers can increase social welfare by adopting legal rules that lead to results that would happen if there were no transaction costs. On the other hand, lawmakers may believe that property development is socially beneficial only if new builders internalize the external costs of their construction to ensure that the benefits of new construction are not outweighed by harm to property owners who built first.

In debating which rule is best, the parties will argue about whether transaction costs are present and how high they are. When a situation involves only two parties, one side may focus on their interests exclusively while the other side may argue that the legal rule choice affects third parties whose interests should be added to the cost-benefit calculus. Those third-party interests are called externalities. The presence of externalities may substantially increase transaction costs since it would be difficult or impossible for all the owners in the neighbor affected by the construction to get together to bargain to a mutually-advantageous result.

One side may also argue that transaction costs are low when there are only two parties because they can talk until they reach agreement, and even if transaction costs are high, letting the parties negotiate is arguably less costly than allowing them to file a lawsuit and give the decision to a judge or jury. The administrative costs of court proceedings to assess liability arguably outweigh the costs of market transactions. The other side may respond that the administrative costs of lawsuits are well worth if it they are based on legal rules designed to discourage socially harmful behavior.

> Are transaction costs low or high?
>
> Are the administrative costs of litigation higher or lower than the market costs of transacting?

When transaction costs prevent the parties from bargaining to achieve the efficient result that maximizes their joint welfare, two strategies are possible for judges crafting legal rules. One is to adopt a legal rule that mimics the result the parties would likely come to if there were no transaction costs. A second, alternative strategy is to shape legal rules that minimize transaction costs, making bargaining easier. One way to minimize transaction costs is to adopt rules that can be applied mechanically so that the parties' rights are clear. Another is to lower the parties' obligations so that they are free to act in a self-interested manner without worrying about liability to someone else.

If transaction costs are high:

Can we lower them by clarifying entitlements or by removing burdensome regulations?

Or should we promote social welfare by adopting legal rules that mimic the outcomes the parties would be likely to agree to in the absence of transaction costs?

The boy in our fireworks hypo may argue that transaction costs would have prevented Massachusetts residents from getting together to bargain with the store to stop its sales to Massachusetts residents. The store would respond that it similarly could not bargain with every Massachusetts resident to induce them to give up their right to sue the store. Perhaps the Governors of the two states could negotiate to reform their laws or create a compromise solution, but of course they would have to convince their own legislatures to go along, and the costs of all that bargaining are enormous. It doesn't look like this is a case where one can argue that transaction costs are low or that we can lower bargaining costs to promote a negotiated solution. The court will need to make a decision whether society is better off allowing states to impose liability on foreign actors that foreseeably cause harm in another state or immunizing actors from liability if they confine their conduct to the state that authorizes their conduct.

§4.3.2 VALUATIONS & THE OFFER-ASKING PROBLEM

How do we identify a dollar amount that measures costs and benefits? There are a variety of ways to do this. One way to measure the value of something is its fair market value: the amount the good would likely sell for on the open market. Fair market value is the point where the demand curve and the supply curve meet. A second way to measure the value of something to someone is to ask how much that person would be willing and able to pay to buy it (the offer price). A third measure of value is to consider the amount one is willing to accept to sell something (the "asking" price.) At least some of the time, offer prices are lower than asking prices, and if that is so, we can compare offer and asking prices in several ways to determine which result maximizes social welfare.

....

Fair market value

Offer price

Asking price

....

Consider the value of a house. If the owner wanted to put it up for sale, she would hire a real estate broker who could advise her on its market value—the price she would be likely to get when she sells it. Let's say the market value of the house is $400,000. Now assume you want to buy her house and you are willing and able to offer her only $200,000. She obviously refuses to sell since she would likely get around $400,000 from someone else if she were interested in selling.

Now assume you are willing and able to offer $500,000. Wouldn't a rational person accept the offer? Since the property is only worth $400,000, the owner could sell it for $500,000 and move into a bigger house or a similar house and save money for retirement. But suppose the owner refuses to sell the house even though you offered more than its market value. Is she being irrational? Of course not. She may not want to sell because she is happy there and has no interest in moving and does not need the extra $100,000 in resources right now.

Now imagine that you offer $1.5 million. Finally, she gives in. That was high enough to induce her to sell the house despite its sentimental value. That means that her asking price (the price at which she was willing to sell) is $1.5 million, assuming that's how much you have to offer her to get her to agree to sell.

Now let's assume you don't have $1.5 million and neither you nor anyone else would spend $1.5 million for a house whose fair market value is only $400,000. Instead, you are willing and able to pay only $200,000 for the house. The owner is unlikely to sell a house worth $400,000 to someone who offers only $200,000 because she is likely to find a buyer that will pay the fair market value for the house, or $400,000.

In this example, we have three different valuations for the house.

- ◻ fair market value = $400,000
- ◻ owner's asking price for the time being = $1,500,000
- ◻ nonowner's offer price = $200,000

What is the "real" value of the house? Who "values" it more? The answer is that there is no "real value." And there is no single way to figure out "who values it more." There are only different ways of measuring the value of the house and who values it more. That is because offer and asking prices may well diverge from fair market value and because asking prices are often higher than both market prices and offer prices.

If you offer me more for my house than its fair market value, I won't sell it to you if I'm not looking to sell it. My asking price is higher than the property's fair market value. I won't sell because I live there, I have no desire to sell, and I have sufficient resources from income and savings not to need the money you are offering me right now. I am also emotionally attached to the house; it is where our daughter grew up.

Although my home does have a great deal of sentimental value, I do imagine some price above market value at which I would be willing to sell. Asking prices are often higher than offer prices. There are various reasons for that. One reason is that my ability to pay limits me in ways that may not affect my need to sell. If I do not own the house, I need to use my own money or borrow to be able to buy the house. My own resources and my wages may not be enough to enable me to afford the house. But if I already own the house and have enough money and wages to live on, I may choose to keep the house rather than sell it.

Consider my neighbor and me. I build a fence where I think the border is and I get my neighbor's approval to do so, but we do not convert our agreement into a written contract. My neighbor sells her house and moves away, and the new neighbor pays to have a survey done and finds out that the fence is not on the boundary recorded in the registry of deeds; it is located on the new neighbor's land. According to the deed, the neighbor owns the three-foot strip on my side of the fence. Trespass law requires me to take down the fence and let my neighbor repossess her ownership rights in the strip, but adverse possession law lets me keep the strip if I have been in exclusive possession of it for twenty years (a period established by state statute).

Is the doctrine of adverse possession a good one? Does it promote social welfare or detract from it? We need to think not just about my neighbor and me but about all neighbors, but we can learn something from our example. If our goal is to promote happiness, satisfaction, well-being, etc., we may do so in several ways. First, we may seek to adopt a rule that fits expectations so that disputes are minimized. Second, we may give people incentives to formalize their arrangements to avoid disputes in the future if those formalities cost less than living with informal understandings. Third, we may assign ownership of the strip to the person likely to value it the most.

If we are trying to figure out who values the strip more, our answers may be different depending on our frame of reference. First, we might ask which of us would buy the strip at an auction. This auction measure of relative value compares the offer prices of both parties. If we assume that we each have equal ability to pay, then the auction measure may help us figure out who values the strip more because it asks which of us is willing to pay more for it. The one willing to pay the most arguably values it the most.[9]

Second, we could start from existing property rights and rules about ownership. Since my fence has been there for twenty years, I own the strip under the doctrine of adverse possession. If my neighbor wants to get the strip back, she has to offer me enough money to get me to sell it to her. A sale will only happen if the non-owners' offer price exceeds my asking price. We can call that comparison the status quo or ownership measure of relative value.

Third, we could imagine what would happen if the property rights were reversed or redistributed. In that case, I would have to offer my neighbor enough to induce her to sell. That measure of relative value would compare my offer price to her asking price. We might call that the redistribution measure of relative value.

Fourth, we could imagine a reverse auction where we want to figure out, not who would pay the most for the strip of land but who we have to pay more to induce them to give it up.

That means there are five different potential ways to figure out which outcome best promotes social welfare.

- ▢ **fair market value**
    - ▢ the amount something would sell for in a competitive market
    - ▢ we compare the joint fair market value of my land and my neighbor's land if I own the strip to the joint fair market value of the two parcels if she owns the strip and we choose the allocation that maximizes the joint fair market value of the two parcels.

---

9. Of course, if we have very unequal economic resources, the willingness to pay measure may simply reflect our relative wealth. Offer prices are based, not just on willingness to pay, but the ability and willingness to pay. A richer person is able to pay more than a poorer person even if the poorer person would get more benefit from it.

- auction value
  - compare the offer prices of both parties
  - give the strip to the person who is willing and able to pay the most
- status quo or "ownership" value
  - use existing law to determine who owns the strip; since adverse possession law gives me title to the strip, I own it.
  - compare the offer price of the nonowner (what the neighbor is willing and able to pay to buy the strip)
  - to the asking price of the owner (what I am willing to accept to sell the strip)
- redistribution value
  - imagine what would happen if ownership were flipped to the nonowner, and the owner had to buy the strip from the nonowner.
  - compare the asking price of the nonowner (my neighbor) to the offer price of the owner (me)
- reverse auction value
  - comparing the asking prices of both parties
  - which of us would ask the most before agreeing to sell the strip?

To understand why these five measures of costs and benefits may lead to different conclusions about which result promotes social welfare, consider an example involving many parties. A factory is spewing smoke and polluting the air and reducing the ability of homeowners in the neighborhood to enjoy their land and avoid medical problems caused by the pollution. Should the factory be free to operate and continue to cause harm or should it be shut down because it causes more harm than good?

One way to address this is to look at the fair market value of the lands of the parties. What rule creates the highest joint market value of the land? If the factory is highly profitable and the houses modest, that may mean that joint fair market value of all the properties in question is maximized if the factory is allowed to continue to operate. Under the market value measure of costs and benefits, the factory should arguably operate.

Alternatively, assume the law allows the factory to operate despite the harm it causes because of legislation designed to protect jobs by eliminating environmental regulations that are thought to cause more harm than good. If the factory has the right to operate without liability, then the homeowners would have to offer the factory enough money to get it to agree to shut down. The factory's asking price is likely to be higher than the homeowners' collective offer price. Under the status quo measure of costs and benefits, the factory should continue to operate.

However, if we reverse the legal rule and give the homeowners the right to shut down the factory because it is harming their use and enjoyment of their property, the opposite result is possible. If we use the redistribution measure (comparing the offer price of the factory to the asking price of the homeowners), the factory owner has to offer the homeowners enough money to get them to agree to continue to suffer from the pollution caused by factory operations. In this case, a single environmental activist could shut the factory down. The factory will not offer more money than it is actually making because that would make it worse off than not operating at all. That means the factory's offer price has a limit. But someone who views pollution as a moral harm may refuse any amount of money to agree to allow it to continue. My soul, she says, is not for sale. Under this redistribution measure and the presence of one activist with the legal right to "just say no," the factory arguably causes more harm than good and it should shut down.

This means that the measure we use to value costs and benefits may affect cost-benefit determinations. While one side in a dispute may focus on market value or auction value, the other side may focus on status quo value or redistribution value. Because these are all legitimate and useful forms of valuation, the result will likely be based on choosing the most appropriate measure of value in the context of the dispute. That can only be done by thorough arguments based on fairness, justice, morality, and rights considerations.

In our fireworks case, it is hard to imagine the victim's family being willing and able to offer the store enough money to get it to shut down. If the store has the right to operate without liability, the store's asking price to stop its sales exceeds the victim's offer price; continued operation is socially beneficial if we measure benefits by using the store's asking price and we measure costs by using the family's offer price. However, if the victim's family has the right to stop the store from operating, we would be comparing the offer price of the store with the asking price of the family. If their experience

Valuation measures

- fair market value
- auction value
- status quo value
- redistribution value
- reverse auction value

led them to view fireworks as too dangerous to be allowed, they may well refuse any amount offered by the store to let it continue to operate. Like the environmental activist, their asking price could exceed their offer price. If they are legally entitled to "just say no" under the redistribution measure of value, then the socially desirable result would be to put the store out of business. Which result promotes social welfare depends on how we decide to value the costs and benefits of the alternative solutions.

§4.4 Presumptions & minimum standards

Default rules are legal rules that define legal entitlements that can be waived by agreement. They are presumptions that help us interpret ambiguous contract language. For example, employment is presumed to be at will; either party can end the relationship at any time. If you want tenure (the right not to be fired without cause), you have to bargain for it and your employment contract has to state that you are protected from discharge without cause.

Mandatory rules, in contrast, are not waivable. They set minimum standards for market relationships. For example, landlords have a duty to provide tenants with heat and hot water and employers have a duty to provide employees with safe working conditions. Any contracts to the contrary are unenforceable. Mandatory rules are sometimes thought to be harmful to society because they are thought to prevent people from making mutually beneficial arrangements, thus leaving people worse off than they would be if they were free to make the agreements they prefer to make.

There are several arguments in favor of mandatory regulations. First, some mandatory regulations are based on considerations of justice, fairness, equality, and liberty. A free and democratic society that treats each person with equal concern and respect will ban agreements inconsistent with its fundamental moral commitments. Oppressive arrangements (such as indentured servitude or subjecting employees to sexual harassment) are immoral or harmful to society. Allowing individuals to waive the right to be protected from oppression would harm society by depriving people of their rights to be protected from illegitimate conduct.

Second, legislatures pass laws that set minimum standards for market relationships. Employment discrimination laws ensure that race does not affect your ability to get a raise. Environmental laws protect us from harmful air and water pollution. Consumer protection laws protect us from fraud and from unfair or deceptive business practices. Regulatory laws set the boundaries within which bargaining can occur. These laws often define things that we should not have to bargain for; they are things we want to take for granted. I should not have to bargain to be free from harassment. I should not have to bargain to be paid a minimum wage. These are things that should go along with legitimate employment relationships.

We may make choices as consumers in markets, but we also make choices as citizens in elections for representatives who enact legislation that sets minimum standards for social and economic relationships. Governments pass laws because (at least some) citizens want them. Minimum standards regulations do not stop us from getting what we want. Minimum standards regulations ensure that we can get what we want when we enter the marketplace by setting minimum standards for market interactions, leaving us free to bargain about other things, rather than having to ask to be treated with common decency.

In the fireworks hypo, the boy may suggest that Massachusetts' democratically elected representatives determined that fireworks harm social welfare; their costs outweigh their benefits. Prohibitive legislation gives people what they want, which is to be safe from ultrahazardous products used by others. New Hampshire law has harmed the people of the Commonwealth of Massachusetts by inflicting blindness upon a little boy. Laws exist to protect us from harm, and society is better off with legislation to protect people from dangerous products like fireworks.

The store may suggest that New Hampshire law promotes social welfare by deregulation that leaves people free to buy and sell fireworks, while Massachusetts law harms social welfare by stopping people from entering mutually beneficial agreements.

SUMMARY OF SOCIAL WELFARE ARGUMENTS

CONSEQUENCES, SOCIAL WELFARE, COSTS & BENEFITS

Social Welfare

- Which rule best promotes the general welfare?
- Which rule promotes social utility, happiness, or human flourishing?

Incentives

- What incentives do the alternative rules create?
- How will people behave if each rule is adopted?

Promotion of Investment

- Which rule best promotes socially desirable economic investment?
- How does each rule stifle desirable development?
- Which rule best discourages socially harmful investment?

Cost Internalization

- Which rule best induces people to internalize the external costs of their activity?
- Which party should bear the burden of paying for the external costs of their conduct?

Cost-Benefit Analysis

- What are the costs and benefits of each rule?
- Which rule promotes the best overall outcome?

Transaction Costs

- Are the costs of bargaining high or low?
- If they are high should the law assign rights to the person who likely values them the most?
  - Or should the law attempt to lower transaction costs by making rights clear to promote bargaining?

Valuations

- Fair market value
- Auction (compare offer prices)
- Status quo (compare owner asking price to nonowner offer price)
- Redistribution (compare nonowner asking price to owner offer price)
- Reverse auction (compare asking prices)

Presumptions & Minimum Standards

- Is the agreement ambiguous or unambiguous?
  - If ambiguous, promote the intent of the parties
  - If ambiguous, promote public policy
- Does the arrangement impose harmful costs on third parties (externalities)?
- Does the agreement violate minimum standards for relationships in a free and democratic society that treats each person with equal concern and respect?
- If either answer is yes, should the agreement contain terms that are nonwaivable to protect third parties or ensure that people get what they are entitled to get out of the arrangement?

PART 3

Rule of Law Arguments

CHAPTER 5.

Democracy & the Rule of Law

§5.1 Lawmaking: principle & compromise

Most of the discussion so far has focused on normative arguments that might be made to judges in crafting common law rules governing interactions among people in social and economic life. On one hand, those discussions are open-ended because they involve arguments of many kinds and because they relate both to principles of fairness and justice and to shaping law to promote the general welfare. On the other hand, arguments to judges are constrained by legislation, precedent, and norms about the appropriate role of judges in a free and democratic society.

Judges are constrained in a variety of ways. First, they are required to enforce statutes passed by Congress and by state legislatures unless those laws violate the federal or state constitutions. Our "republican" form of government gives the people the sovereign power to select representatives who pass laws that promote the general welfare. When a statute applies to a case, we want judges to "enforce the law" as established by elected representatives.

Second, judges follow precedent in common law cases not governed by statute unless there are good reasons to overrule applicable precedents or to distinguish them. This is part of what we mean by the rule of law where we treat like cases alike so people enjoy equal protection of law while being able to plan and avoid unfair surprise. The mandate that people are equal before the law and entitled to the same rights granted to others who are similarly situated is one of the most important checks on judicial power.

Third, judges have to give good reasons to overturn a precedent or to distinguish a prior case. Those reasons are based on values we hold in common in a system that does not establish a governing religion and which is committed to constitutional rights of liberty and equality. The practice of giving reasons and explaining why judicial rulings are consistent with prior law, with enacted statutes, and with the state and federal constitutions constrains judicial discretion.

Legislatures, however, work quite differently. While politicians do give reasons for their votes, they do not engage in the same type of systematic opinion writing and reason giving that constrains what judges can do. Legislators can vote without giving a reason at all. Moreover, they are free to make arguments that may be partisan in nature, at least compared to the types of reasons that judges give. Rather than giving reasons the losing side might accept, legislators may focus on one side of the argument. They may focus on the benefits of a law without acknowledging its costs; they may criticize an opponent's proposed law as costly without acknowledging its benefits. They may champion freedom from regulation without acknowledging the ways they themselves support regulation.

There are better and worse ways of arguing in politics. Our political system would be better off if political debates adopted some of the methods of civil discourse that lawyers have developed for use in the court system, especially the norm of showing respect for the other side and willingness to acknowledge legitimate counterarguments.

On the other hand, there are also benefits to a freewheeling form of debate in the political world. People are free in that setting to paint a vivid picture of their objections to laws they deem unjust or unwise, and to describe the kind of world they want us to have. In addition, statutes may be limited in scope, solving part of a problem but not the whole. That kind of inconsistency is allowed in the world of politics and is problematic in the judicial sphere of common law development where consistency and coherence are central to judicial reasoning.

In thinking about the appropriate role of judges in a free and democratic system, it is important to understand the difference between the roles of state judges and federal judges. The Supreme Court decided in 1935 that federal courts are limited to enforcing federal and state statutes and constitutions, as well as state common law. Federal judges are generally not allowed to create or to develop federal common law governing relations among persons.[1] In contrast, state judges have the power to adjudicate cases even when they are not governed by any statute. State judges create, shape, implement, and change common law rules to govern social relationships, such as the law of property, contracts, torts, and family law, when no statute covers the issue.

This difference between federal and state courts affects the way they make decisions. After the 1938 *Erie* decision,[2] federal courts that find that the plaintiff has no rights under federal or state statutes generally dismiss the plaintiff's complaint unless the plaintiff can show she has rights under state common law. In contrast, when a state judge is confronted with a case not governed by any federal or state statute or any state common law rule, the judge will not just dismiss the complaint on the ground that no law provides relief to the plaintiff. Rather, state judges must decide the case under state common law. Either the plaintiff is right, and she has a common law claim against the defendant, or the defendant is right, and the court should rule that defendant's actions did not violate the plaintiff's common law rights. Either way, the state judge asked to decide the case must craft a common law rule.

> Federal judges do not make common law (generally) so they must dismiss the complaint if they find no law that grants rights to the plaintiff
>
> In contrast, state judges craft common law rules to decide cases that come before them so they must decide whether or not to grant plaintiff common law rights

Because state judges are empowered to create common law rules, their relation to the legislature is different from that of federal judges to Congress. Federal judges have less power to make law than state judges do. When a federal judge in Boston faces a case that involves common law rights under Massachusetts law, the judge's job is to guess what the state supreme court would want her to do. When the state supreme court is addressing the same case, it does not predict what it itself will do; rather, it interprets the common law of Massachusetts and may reshape it, reconcile competing lines of precedent, and even overrule cases or adopt new rules of common law. When you hear people say that judges should not

---

1. Two major exceptions are federal Indian law and maritime law.
2. Erie R.R. v. Tompkins, 304 U.S. 64 (1938).

make law, we need to take that with a grain of salt if we are talking about the role of state judges in our legal system. There is no question that state judges make law when they adjudicate a dispute under common law. That does not mean state judges do not feel constrained by precedents created by judges in the past, but it does mean that they are empowered to decide what the common law of the state is, at least until the legislature overrules them by passing a statute. While state judges are responsible for state common law, we do have debates about the appropriate relationship between state judges and state legislatures when state judges exercise their common law powers.

§5.2 Institutional roles

We sometimes hear it said that "judges should apply the law rather than make it." In reality, there is no way for judges to do their job—to interpret precedents or statutes or constitutional texts—without exercising judgment. If it were obvious what the law was, we would not need a lawsuit to determine what the rules are and how they apply to specific cases. When there are good arguments for competing interpretations of law, judges have no choice but to make reasoned judgments and defend their choices as best they can. At the same time, lawyers and citizens have spirited debates about the appropriate way for judges to do this. Institutional role arguments concern competing interpretations of the role of judges in a free and democratic society.

A judge who veers too far from either precedent or legislative policy faces the possibility of being called a judicial activist who is usurping the lawmaking role of the legislature. When people criticize judges for being judicial activists, they usually are claiming that those judges have exceeded the legitimate scope of their authority. These claims may be of several types, including: (a) cases where judges change the law (either common law or constitutional law); (b) cases where judges strike down statutes as unconstitutional and thereby override the will of the legislature; or (c) cases where judges explain their decisions in terms of values, arguments, policies, and competing considerations rather than claiming they are simply "calling balls and strikes" and deferring to the clear mandate of some source of law. Those who criticize judges for being activist are implicitly calling for judges to exercise judicial restraint.

It is common to hear nominees for the Supreme Court vowing not to make law. They usually mean that they will enforce statutory provisions as written and defer to the clear meaning of constitutional clauses. They feel pressure to make this assertion because democratic societies vest legislative authority in elected representatives and the main job of judges is to interpret and apply the laws made by the legislature. At the same time, one could only refrain from "making law" if the law were clear and easily discernible. But statutes are often ambiguous and constitutional provisions are by their very nature general and in need of interpretation. When statutes and constitutional provisions are ambiguous, judges have no choice but to listen to competing arguments and engage in judgment as best they can.

When a case involves state judges interpreting the common law, arguments about judicial activism and restraint have a somewhat different character. If a rule is a common law rule, that means it was made by some judge in the past. Asking judges not to make law is problematic in this context because the law in question is one that was actually made by judges. The argument for judicial restraint here usually means that judges should enforce precedents made by prior judges until those rules are changed by the legislature through a new statute.

The problem with this kind of judicial restraint is that a judge who applies old common law rules mechanically and without attention to changing social values and conditions or existing legislative policy faces the possibility of being accused being unjust or foolish. Rulings that strike the general public as unwise or unfair undermine respect for the legal system. Enforcing old common law rules that violate contemporary values or social conditions or current legislative policy may subject judges to the accusation that they are not applying the law in a fair or sensible manner. For that reason, judges do change common law rules over time to modernize them and to ensure that they fit current values, conditions, and legislative policies.

Consider the implied warranty of habitability. This common law rule says that residential landlords have an implied contractual duty to provide tenants with housing that is safe, habitable, and consistent with the local building code. Judges created that doctrine in the middle of the twentieth century. They did so by overruling precedents that said that landlords have no contractual duty to provide safe and habitable premises. On the contrary, they held that a landlord who violates the housing code has breached the lease agreement, giving the tenant the right to either stop paying rent, pay a reduced rent to reflect the loss of housing services, and continue to live in the apartment until it is fixed or to repudiate the lease and move out before the end of the lease term.

When judges created this new common law rule, did they engage in inappropriate judicial activism or did they act in an appropriate restrained manner by shaping the common law to reflect current legislative policy and the justified expectations of landlords and tenants?

The landlord may argue that the judges who gave tenants the right to reduced rent when the landlord is violating the housing code engaged in a form of inappropriate judicial activism. The argument for judicial restraint here is that the state legislature had passed a building code and the local government a housing code but neither of those laws gave tenants the right to stop paying rent if landlords violate them. The appropriate body to change the law is arguably the state legislature or the municipal government. If legislators have acted in an area by passing statutes or regulations, judges should enforce the laws they have written rather than rewriting them.

There are two different reasons for engaging in judicial restraint. First, the landlord may argue that legislators are the primary lawmakers in a democracy while judges generally apply the laws made by those lawmakers. The appropriate institutional role of judges is to defer to legislators. Judges can nudge legislators by writing opinions that suggest that legislators should update laws to address issues the legislature has not addressed, but judges should not create rights beyond what is contained in legislation or common law precedents. New laws enacted by legislatures will have more popular support than new rules made by judges since legislatures are more accountable to voters.

Institutional roles:

Defer to the legislature to make policy (judicial restraint) or

Exercise common law authority to promote the parties' rights (judicial activism or responsibility) knowing the legislature is free to overrule the court by passing a statute

Second, the landlord will argue that legislatures are more competent than judges at investigating facts, obtaining expert judgments, and canvassing community desires and beliefs. New regulations should go through this process, rather than just through litigation in court. Judges must base their rulings on evidence presented by the parties; they have no power to hold hearings, call in witnesses, or hire staffs to make reports about the best public policies. Legislatures have greater competence at determining the social effects of legal rules and in crafting appropriate political compromises. Judges, on the other hand, have to accept whatever evidence is presented in court and are limited to adjudicating the controversy before them. Given the legislature's superior competence in lawmaking, judges should refrain from changing the law or modernizing it.

Legislatures may be more competent than judges
- to find out what the facts are
- to determine the social consequences of different regulations by expert testimony
- to make appropriate political compromises

But judges know how to shape common law rules to achieve fair and sensible outcomes in disputes that fit current social values, norms, conditions, and legislation

The tenants will argue, in contrast, that modernizing common law rules is both consistent with the judicial role and within the competence of judges. It is not impermissibly activist for a judge to conclude, after hearing arguments on both sides, that a rule of law laid down one hundred years ago no longer seems fair, consistent with justified expectations, or congruent with policies evident in current legislation. Nor does it make sense to argue that the judge should not make law when we are talking about a common law rule that was made by a judge or judges in the past. Judges today are no less competent to make determinations of fairness and welfare than were judges in the past.

When one party asks the judge to modernize a common law rule, the judge will be making law whichever way she goes. When someone goes to court to complain that she has been wronged by someone else, the judge has no alternative to deciding whether that claim is valid or not. If the judge denies the victim a remedy based on a precedent from long ago, the judge is effectively making law by choosing to enforce the existing common law rule. By applying the precedent, the judge is saying what the common law is. Because state judges are empowered to shape and interpret common law, a judicial refusal to modernize the common law is no less "activist" than a decision to overrule the precedent and provide a claim for the victim that the common law had not previously recognized.

The tenant will argue that judges routinely and appropriately overrule precedent when social values, conditions, and laws have changed. The housing code and the building code place obligations on landlords to maintain the rental property in a habitable manner. Those statutes and regulations change the legal and moral context within which landlords and tenants bargain. If the court were to rule that the landlord may violate the housing code and that this does not violate the tenant's rights, the judge will be not be acting in a restrained manner but rather in defiance of the statutes and ordinances that define the obligations of landlords. In fact, it is arguably an exercise of judicial restraint for the judge to define the landlord's contractual obligations by reference to existing statutes that set minimum standards for residential rental housing. And even if there were no housing code, judges have changed the common law over time to keep it consistent with current norms, policies, customs, and laws so as to protect justified expectations and to promote fair outcomes under current community standards.

The tenant will also argue that judges are competent to modernize common law rules. They do so, not in an arbitrary manner, but by looking at legislative policy, the relation between the rule being decided and other rules of law so that the law is consistent and coherent, and evolving social values and attitudes and conditions. In addition, it is useful for judges to modernize old rules that were made by judges and that the legislatures have not focused on. The problem of nonenforcement of the housing code and whether tenants should be required to continue to pay rent when their property is not habitable may never have come to the legislature's attention. The ability of any person to make a claim against another person in court means that ordinary people have the power to make their voices heard by impartial judges even though they may not be able to attract the attention of the legislature. The judge must respond by crafting or interpreting legal rules, and a ruling for the defendant is as much a ruling of law as is one for the plaintiff. That means that judges make law whether or not they recognize new rights.

> Judges may be more competent than legislatures to
>
> – adjudicate the particularities of specific cases
> – to learn about and respond to problems that have not come to the legislature's attention
> – to shape rules that seek to show respect to both sides

Courts have an obligation to answer the question one way or another. Either the landlord's failure to repair the premises constitutes a breach of contract or it does not. If the judge enforces precedent and finds no breach of contract, it is basing its ruling on a decision made by another judge long ago. There is no reason to believe that judges in the past were more competent than today's judges. If the judge is not competent to determine the effects of overturning precedent, neither is the judge competent to determine the effects of applying the precedent. And in either case, the legislature is free to overrule the judge, either by giving the tenants the right to withhold rent if the landlord fails to provide habitable housing or by denying them that remedy. A change in the common law in no way disables the legislature from deciding how such cases should be treated by passing new legislation to restore the old common law rule and codify it in a statute.

CHAPTER **6.**

Precedent

§6.1 Experience & treating like cases alike

"The life of the law has not been logic; it has been experience," wrote Justice Oliver Wendell Holmes Jr. He went on to say:

> The felt necessities of the time, the prevalent moral and political theories, intuitions of public policy, avowed or unconscious, even the prejudices which judges share with their fellow-men, have had a good deal more to do than the syllogism in determining the rules by which men should be governed. The law embodies the story of a nation's development through many centuries, and it cannot be dealt with as if it contained only the axioms and corollaries of a book of mathematics.[1]

Holmes did not mean that law is illogical or that reason has no role in the legal system. What he meant is that we learn from experience and that human life is too complicated to be reduced to rigid rules that do not take account of social context, as well as evolving historical conditions and values.

On one hand, learning from experience means that custom and precedent matter. First of all, they provide stability. We do

---

1. Oliver Wendell Holmes, Jr. *The Common Law* 1 (1881).

things a certain way and we are able to negotiate daily life because we know what to expect. Both social custom and judicial precedents give us a basis for our expectations so that we can live our lives knowing what is expected of us and what we can expect of others. We learn from experience and we want people to be able to rely on the existing legal rules in planning their behavior so they are not unfairly surprised by changes in the law. Second, if we have solved a problem already, it makes sense to use the tried and true solution rather than to start from scratch. We need good reasons to depart from prior decisions about which rules are fair and effective.

On the other hand, learning from experience means that we are not imprisoned by prior custom or precedent. New facts and new norms can change how we evaluate fact situations and legal rules. We may come to believe we were mistaken and that we need new rules that better attune to current social circumstances and values. Experience may give us reason to rely on precedent, but it also gives us reason to change.[2]

The U.S. legal system empowers judges to interpret statutes and constitutions, but it also gives state judges the power to settle disputes not governed by any state or federal statute or regulation. Every state allows people to sue others to claim that they have been wronged and to seek civil recourse. The wrong may be an injury from negligent conduct, from breach of contract, from infringement of property rights, or something else. Appellate courts write judicial opinions that explain the facts of the case, the alternative rules that were considered, the rule that is adopted with reasons why it was adopted, the way the rule applies to the case itself, and how the case should be resolved, either by dismissal, payment of damages, or a court order to the parties to act in a manner consistent with the legal rule that is announced.

Judicial opinions create precedents that guide cases to be decided in the future. Our common law system gives judges the power to make law by resolving civil disputes and announcing rules of law to govern them—and like cases that arise in the future. Judge-made common law rules are rules of law as much as rules laid down by legislatures in statutes.

Follow precedent because:
We learn from experience
So we can plan
So like cases are treated alike
and we are treated equally

2. For more on these competing views of precedent, *see* Karl N. Llewellyn, *The Bramble Bush: The Classic Lectures on the Law and Law School* (Oxford U. Press ed., 2008) (originally published as *The Bramble Bush: On Our Law and Its Study* (1930)).

When a case comes before a state court, the lawyers for the parties seek to establish the facts (what happened and who did what to whom) and the governing state law. The lawyers may argue about which legal rule governs the situation or how to interpret any existing rules established in prior cases. If a case is exactly like one decided in the past, then, all things being equal, the court will decide the new case in the same way the old case was decided. That is because fairness demands that we treat like cases alike. If a court has determined that a rule of law appropriately governs a situation, then everyone in similar circumstances has the right to the benefits of the same rule. On the other hand, if we come to view an existing common law rule as unfair or detrimental to society, we are not imprisoned by our prior practices. We can treat people equally by adopting a new rule that better protects everyone's rights.

§6.2 Applying & distinguishing precedent

When a case is just like a previously decided case, courts apply precedent unless they are convinced not to do so. The prior case establishes a rule of law that governs similar situations in the future, creating a precedent on which both citizens and judges can rely. Lawyers are able to advise clients about the rules governing their conduct because the law clearly answers many questions about our rights and obligations to other people. But life is complicated, and often the problem before us is different in certain respects from the problem faced in the case that established the precedent. What do we do then?

If the precedent says that the plaintiff wins and the defendant loses, the plaintiff's lawyer in a new case will want the court to apply the precedent to this dispute and will argue that this case is just like the precedent. She will do this by identifying the relevant facts that are the same and explaining why any facts that are different do not provide reasons to treat this case differently. If the plaintiff had a right to win in the earlier case, the plaintiff in this case has the same right. The plaintiff will give normative reasons why the factual differences between the two cases do not matter. She will argue that they create a distinction without a difference.

In contrast, the defendant will try to identify how the facts of the current dispute are different from those in the precedent or she will explain why the two cases arise in different social contexts. She will need to explain why those facts matter and give reasons why the rule applied in the prior case should not be applied here. She will try to distinguish the precedent. The converse of treating like cases alike is that cases that are not alike in relevant ways should be treated differently. For this to happen, the defendant must not only point to factual or contextual differences, but she must explain why those differences matter. She must give normative reasons (like those explored in chapters 3 & 4) to treat the two cases differently; that means she must explain why the new facts matter and justify a different result.

> To distinguish a prior case or precedent:
> – Show why the facts of the precedent are different from those in the current dispute
> – And explain why that factual difference matters
>
> To show why a case should not be distinguished, explain why those factual differences do not provide a good reason to treat the current dispute differently from the precedent

For example, in the case of *Friendswood Development Co. v. Smith-Southwest Industries, Inc.,*[3] a subsidiary of Exxon was withdrawing groundwater[4] from beneath its property for sale to industrial users. Prior cases had held that owners may withdraw groundwater from their property through wells on their own land even if doing so means that they are also drawing water away from underneath neighboring property. That is because it is impossible to ensure that the water you produce from a well on your land comes only from water located beneath the surface of your land. Water flows and seeps through soil and rock; groundwater does not respect boundaries. The problem, however, was that Exxon was taking so much water that it was undermining subjacent support[5] for neighboring land. The water that permeated the ground of the neighbors helped sustain the dirt that supported the surface, where homes and businesses were located. The neighboring owners sued Exxon because its actions in withdrawing water from its own land were sinking their homes and could eventually render them dangerous and uninhabitable.

---

3. 576 S.W.2d 21 (Tex. 1978).

4. Groundwater is water that is diffused beneath the surface of land that the landowner can withdraw using a well.

5. "Subjacent" support refers to support for land that comes from beneath it. Imagine a mining company that extracts minerals from beneath the surface to such an extent that the surface has no support and caves in. That is what is meant by undermining subjacent support for the surface land.

Exxon argued that the plaintiffs had no rights. Since it had already been established in a prior case that Exxon had the right to withdraw water from beneath its land even if this drew water from neighboring lands, it was only doing what it was legally entitled to do. Moreover, it relied on those precedents when it decided to invest in withdrawing all that water and selling it to customers who needed it; the precedents held that it would not be liable for withdrawing water from neighboring land if it acted only on its own land. To change the rule after Exxon relied on it when making an investment would unfairly surprise an actor who acted in accord with existing legal rules.

The neighbors argued that the issue in this case was fundamentally different from the issue in the prior cases. Those prior cases involved disputes about who owns the water beneath the surface. One rule would say that you own the groundwater beneath your land and hydrologists can give scientific evidence about the amount and location of groundwater so that those who withdraw water and sell it should apportion the profits based on the amount of water drawn from beneath each parcel of land. The courts had rejected that rule because it was too cumbersome, adopting instead a rule of first use: whoever withdraws the water first owns it even if they are drawing water from neighboring land.

This case, the neighbors argued, is not about who owns the water; rather, it is about whether you are allowed to withdraw so much water that you wind up harming your neighbor's land. According to the plaintiffs, the fact that the withdrawals were undermining support for the surface land made this case distinguishable from the precedent. Moreover, there were good reasons to treat the two cases differently. Ordinary water withdrawal does not harm the community because the first use rule gives an incentive to withdraw the water first, as long as it is not wasted, and it makes the water available for sale and use by the community. It increases property values rather than harming them. Here harms are being caused by the water withdrawal. Moreover, as the dissenting judge argued, "many things, though lawful, when done to excess become remediable."[6] Giving an owner the right to harvest the water is different from giving an owner the freedom to sink the entire city "to the bottom of Galveston Bay."[7]

_____

6. 576 S.W.2d at 33.

7. *Id.*

§6.3 Reconciling conflicting precedents

The plaintiffs in *Friendswood* made a second argument. In addition to trying to distinguish their case from prior cases, they appealed to other rules
of law that they claimed were directly applicable to their situation or that
should be extended to apply to their case. The plaintiffs argued that precedents had established the principle that
owners have a right to not have their land
undermined in any way by construction
on neighboring land. Prior cases had established the rule that allows owners to
dig on their own properties to be able to
construct homes but required them to
take measures to protect neighboring land
from falling into the hole. Therefore land-
owners are obliged to provide support for
adjacent land so that the excavation on their own property does not harm
their neighbor's property. Likewise, owners have a fundamental right to
have their land in its natural state remain free from harm by actions on
neighboring land.

> When two rules seem to apply to
> a case and have opposite
> outcomes:
> – Interpret one rule broadly to
>   cover the facts of the case
> – Interpret the other rule
>   narrowly so it does not apply
>   to the case

Although prior cases had addressed the issue of lateral support for land
(support along the side of the land) and the *Friendswood* case concerned
subjacent support (support from underneath), the plaintiffs argued that
that is a distinction without a difference. Rather than reading the prior cases
narrowly as establishing a rule about lateral support of land, they argued
that we should read them broadly as establishing a right to the support of
land, period, whether lateral or subjacent or otherwise. You are free to build
on your own land as long as you leave my land alone. That norm gives a
good reason to treat the lateral support precedent broadly. Conversely, the
rule that authorizes withdrawal of water arguably applies only to disputes
about water ownership; it does not apply when water withdrawal undermines neighboring land. Reading the land support precedents broadly and
the water rights precedents narrowly would mean that this case is governed
not by the rule that allows withdrawal of water from neighboring land, but
by the rule that prohibits harm to neighboring land.

The defendant will answer that this case is squarely governed by the
prior rules about withdrawal of water and that prior rules about lateral

support are not relevant to a case about subjacent support. It will want the rule about withdrawal of water to be interpreted broadly to encompass withdrawal even when it harms neighboring land support while it will argue that the prior cases about support of land should be interpreted narrowly so they only apply to lateral support of land and not to subjacent support. This difference may make sense because it is easy to provide lateral support for neighboring land during construction: just build a retaining wall in your excavation so neighboring land stays in place. It is not easy to refrain from withdrawing groundwater from neighboring land when you take water from your own land by producing water from a well. And we want to encourage the withdrawal of water needed for industrial and residential uses so it can be used or sold to those who need it. There are good reasons to distinguish lateral support cases from subjacent support cases. That means that prior cases giving a right to lateral support of land should not extend to issues involving subjacent support, especially when there is a competing rule of law giving owners the right to freely withdraw water from wells on their own land even if they draw water from their neighbor's land.

As it turns out, the judges on the Texas Supreme Court rejected all these arguments, instead ruling that this was a case of first impression. It interpreted the groundwater rules narrowly since they did not involve harm to neighboring land and they also interpreted the rules about lateral support narrowly so they did not govern a case concerning subjacent support. For that reason, the court found that this was a fact situation it had never faced before and no prior precedents had adopted a common law rule governing cases like this. They had no choice but to craft a new common law rule governing water withdrawal that undermines subjacent support of neighboring land, show how it fit with prior precedents, and give normative reasons why it is both fair and good for society.[8]

------

8. In case you are interested, the court held that disputes between neighbors about noise or pollution are governed by rules that prevent owners from acting unreasonably to cause substantial harm to neighboring property and that this third set of rules should be extended to apply to water withdrawal that undermines subjacent support for neighboring land. Owners are free to use their own land if they do so in a reasonable manner. The court then interpreted that rule to provide broad power to withdraw water and limited liability to the neighbors to cases where the neighbors could prove that the excavator was acting negligently.

§6.4 Overruling precedents

"It is revolting to have no better reason for a rule of law than that so it was laid down in the time of Henry IV," wrote Justice Oliver Wendell Holmes, Jr. He went on: "It is still more revolting if the grounds upon which it was laid down have vanished long since, and the rule simply persists from blind imitation of the past."[9] We have seen that there are good reasons to follow precedent. But it is also true that times change; both values and social conditions evolve over time. When a case is easy, and an existing legal rule governs it, we just apply the rule. But when a case is hard—when someone comes up with a plausible argument about why the old rule is unfair or harmful to society—we cannot just apply the old rule without justifying doing so. We need to give reasons why the old rule still works and does not deprive anyone of their rights.

When a case is hard, sometimes the courts change the law by overruling precedents that established rules we can no longer live with. As we have seen, until the last quarter of the twentieth century, residential landlords had no contractual obligations to repair the premises or keep them up to standards set by housing codes. States had passed statutes setting minimum standards for building construction, and municipalities had adopted ordinances regulating rental housing to ensure that it is safe and habitable, but those laws were not thought to have any effect on contractual obligations that landlords have to tenants. Instead, the courts required tenants to continue paying rent even if they had no heat in the middle of winter and had to move out. In addition, courts interpreted the covenants in the lease to be independent of each other; even if the lease contained an express promise by the landlord to comply with the housing code, a breach of that covenant did not empower the tenant to stop paying rent or to get out of the lease and move elsewhere, even if the apartment was not habitable. The tenant's only remedy was to call the housing inspector and seek administrative enforcement of the housing code or sue the landlord for a court order to repair the premises. But the tenant still had to pay rent for the rest of the lease term.

In the late 1960s and 1970s, courts in the US changed the law. The first cases to do so were decided in Hawai'i and New Jersey in 1969.[10] But the

---

9. Oliver Wendell Holmes, Jr. *The Path of the Law,* 10 Harv. L. Rev. 457, 469 (1897)

10. Lemle v. Breeden, 462 P.2d 470 (Haw. 1969); Reste Realty Corp. v. Cooper, 251 A.2d 268 (N.J. 1968).

case that had the most impact was *Javins v. First National Realty Corp.*[11] in a persuasive opinion written by Judge J. Skelly Wright. That case involved apartment buildings that had hundreds of housing code violations. Administrative enforcement of the housing codes had not been effective and the tenants' rights to safe housing were being ignored. Importantly, both social conditions and values had changed since the time when landlords were held to have no maintenance duties.

Judge Wright explained that the old rule of law was created when we were an agricultural society where the tenant was most interested in access to the landlord's land. The building was secondary, and it was the norm that the tenant would maintain his own house and was fully capable of doing so. Those social conditions were long gone by 1970. Not only are tenants not capable of maintaining their own buildings (most lack the expertise), but they are not legally entitled to do so when they live in apartments with shared facilities. Tenants have the right to possess their own apartments and to traverse common areas, but they do not have the right to replace facilities that service the whole building; that is the landlord's prerogative. Because tenants are dependent on the landlord to fix the premises, the social conditions that may have justified the "no duty to repair" rule were missing in the case of modern apartment buildings.

In addition to changed social conditions, norms had changed. There were housing codes that set minimum standards for safety in residential housing, and consumer protection laws gave consumers rights to goods that were safe and worked as advertised. Moreover, while property law made covenants independent in leases, contract law made other kinds of promises contingent on performance by the other side. If I promise to buy your old car on condition that you fix a problem with it, and you fail to do that, then I am no longer obligated to go through with the deal. Our mutual promises are *dependent* on each other.

There are reasons for mutual covenants to be independent in most cases involving real property. If the deed to my house has a restriction limiting my property to residential use, I am obligated to comply with that restriction even if my neighbor violates a similar restriction in her deed that is intended to benefit my property. My remedy is not to be released from my own obligation to my neighbor but to sue my neighbor to get a court order forcing her to comply with the restriction in her deed. But landlord/tenant

---

11. 428 F.2d 1071 (D.C. Cir. 1970).

relationships are different. Should a tenant be required to keep paying rent for an apartment if the building burns down? If what matters is access to the land, then the answer is yes; if what matters is access to a living space with associated services like heat and hot water, the answer is no. A tenant should not be required to keep paying rent for an apartment she can no longer occupy.

The *Javins* decision overruled prior cases that had given landlords the right to keep collecting rent even if the landlord was not providing the services the landlord had promised to provide. The court found that the housing code was an implied term in the lease agreement. A promise to provide housing in an apartment does not only mean that the landlord will not have you arrested for trespass if you enter the apartment but that the apartment will have the services we customarily associate with apartment living, including heat, hot water, a kitchen, a bathroom, windows that are not broken, working locks on the doors, premises free from pests, etc. Tenants do not have to bargain for these things; they are mandatory terms in the lease agreement. Minimum standards set by statute, regulation, and ordinance define things we have a right to expect when we rent an apartment. A landlord who fails to repair the premises has therefore broken her own promise. The new rule adopted in *Javins* gave tenants the right to stop paying for services the landlord was no longer providing. It also gave tenants the right to move out before the end of the lease term or to obtain a court order that the landlord repair the premises. The new rule also empowered judges to allow tenants to pay a reduced rent for the period when the apartment was uninhabitable or unhealthy.

After the *Javins* decision, the courts in state after state adopted a similar rule. Today almost every state has changed the law. Moreover, legislatures were impressed by the reasoning in Judge Wright's opinion, and many amended their statutes to codify the new common law rules requiring landlords to provide habitable housing as a condition of renting the property.

When courts overrule precedents, what happens to the principle of treating like cases alike? Our goal is not just to treat like cases alike but to treat like cases alike under rules that are fair and that promote social welfare. If social conditions or values have changed—or if new legislation has been passed, like housing codes—we want the rules in force to be coherent with other laws and with contemporary values and conditions. Changes in common law ensure that the law continues to be just and wise rather than relegating us to rules that no longer meet our sense of justice or that have undesirable social consequences. And when judges change common law rules, legislatures remain free to overrule them if they disagree by passing statutes that restore the old rules.

CHAPTER 7.

Rules & Standards

§7.1 Predictable rules, flexible standards

Some legal rules are mechanical and rigid, like the one that says "you cannot vote until you are 18 years old." Most people know when they were born and both they and election officials can comply with that rule easily. You either are or are not above 18 years old.

Other legal rules (called standards) require judgment to apply them, like the rule that makes us liable for injuries we cause to other people if we act negligently. Applying that rule requires judging whether we acted reasonably. We cannot apply standards without making normative judgments. Imagine if the law only allowed "mature people" to vote. A "maturity" rule would require contextualized judgments, both by individuals who must determine whether they will be breaking the law if they go to the voting booth and by officials who must determine whether a person is entitled to vote.

> Rules can be applied mechanically
>
> Standards require judgment

Rules and standards have opposite costs and benefits. First is the issue of predictability. Rigid rules tend to be more predictable and easier to apply than flexible standards. Standards are arguably less predictable because they require judgments about both facts and values.

Predictability is a good thing for several reasons. First, rigid rules mean that people can easily tell what rights and obligations they have. That makes it easy for people to obey the law and to plan their conduct in reliance on those rules. It gives people a basis for expecting how other people are going to act as well. It protects them from the unfair surprise that occurs if they are charged with breaking a rule they did not know existed.

Predictable rules

– help us plan our conduct to comply with the law
– ensure like cases are treated alike
– prevent unfair surprise
– control judicial discretion

Second, rigid rules ensure that like cases are treated alike. Because standards require judgment, different judges may judge the same case differently since they interpret the standard in different ways. They themselves may even be inconsistent over time in how they adjudicate cases. Rules ensure equal protection of law and they avoid the unfairness that occurs when some people are deprived of the benefits of rules that have been extended to others. Rules achieve this kind of consistency by constraining judicial discretion.

On the other hand, rigid rules create problems as well as benefits. The main problem is rigidity. The very thing that makes rules predictable may deprive them of the ability to account for new circumstances or competing values. A rule that allows an owner to dig a well on her own land and withdraw groundwater from neighboring land could enable an owner to destroy everyone else's property in the entire city, if rigidly applied under the circumstances of the *Friendswood* case. If the rule allowed owners to withdraw water in a reasonable manner, then the courts could distinguish the *Friendswood* case from earlier case law and find that withdrawal of water from wells is usually reasonable, but unreasonable if it undermines subjacent support for neighboring lands and is so extensive that it will destroy an entire neighborhood.

Rules are predictable but may be overly rigid reaching results that are unfair

Conventional wisdom teaches that rules are predictable but over- and under-inclusive, while standards are flexible but less predictable. Because rules generalize, there will be some cases that reach "wrong" results when the rule applies to a case. We are not smart enough to get the rules exactly right; moreover, our moral intuitions and policy goals are too complex to be reduced to rigid, easily administrable rules. The generalizations provided by rules come at the cost of accuracy; we use them because the benefits of predictability often outweigh the costs of imprecision. But even the best-crafted rules may lead to results that seem unfair. Rigid application of rules may therefore lessen confidence in the legal system and even reduce incentives to voluntarily comply with law.

Rules may be predictable but also over- and under-inclusive, creating injustice in some cases

Standards are flexible but often far less predictable than rules

Rules have another problem; they may allow an unscrupulous person to "walk the line." If one is acting within the scope of a rule and knows that it will be applied mechanically, then one can be certain there will be no legal sanction for one's conduct. Rules grant the luxury of indifference. They invite self-interested persons to act like Holmes's "bad man" and go forward with harmful but lawful conduct.[1]

Rules let the "bad man" walk the line

Standards promote attentiveness to others

In contrast, standards promote attentiveness to the effects of one's actions on others. Their vagueness gives actors incentives to imagine how their conduct will be judged by others, thus inducing actors to avoid conduct that judges or juries will view with disfavor. For this reason, standards may promote moral introspection and justification. Standards allow us to consider all relevant factors; they allow decision makers to come to what they consider the right result in particular cases. By exercising judgment under a covering standard, judges can avoid the unfair results mandated by rigid rules, as well as the inefficiencies that result from applying a rule even when its benefits are outweighed by its costs.

This potential increase in fairness and efficiency arguably comes at the cost of predictability; rather than mechanical application of a clear rule, individuals must "guess" what judges will do when confronted with a case governed by a standard. By requiring judgment, standards therefore make

---

1. Justice Oliver Wendell Holmes, Jr. wrote an influential article in which he explained that he was looking at the law as a "bad man" who "cares only for the material consequences" that come from acting as one pleases. Oliver Wendell Holmes, *The Path of the Law,* 10 Harv. L. Rev. 457, 459 (1897). That perspective eschews moral inquiry and only focuses on whether one will or will not be subjected to legal sanction for one's conduct.

it harder for individuals to plan, for lawyers to advise clients about their rights, and for judges to decide cases. Standards increase the possibility that like cases will not be treated alike and that judges may exercise inappropriate favoritism. Standards may not only mire private actors in uncertainty but lower confidence in the court system and the rule of law.

Both rules and standards require individuals to think before they act but they do so in different ways. Rules require actors to be attentive to what is prohibited, but standards require actors to engage in moral reflection to determine whether they could justify their actions to those affected by them or to those empowered to judge them.

§7.2 Why rules are flexible

The standard argument that rules gain predictability at the cost of flexibility is overstated. The *Friendswood* case discussed in chapter 6 involved a number of clear, seemingly rigid rules: (1) owners are free to withdraw groundwater from wells on their own land even if it draws water away from beneath neighboring land; and (2) owners have a duty to excavate in a manner that provides support for neighboring land. We saw, however, that these rules could not be applied without interpretation. Did the privilege to withdraw water extend to destroying the subsurface of the neighbor's land? Did the duty to provide support for land limit the freedom to withdraw water when that undermined subjacent support for land rather than lateral support? Rules do not determine their own scope; judges must make normative judgments about how broadly or narrowly to interpret them. Because cases can be distinguished and precedents can be overruled, judges cannot avoid judgments in hard cases even if they are confronted with rigid rules.

When a case is hard, rules do not determine their own scope

They must be interpreted to determine whether they apply to a given fact situation

Precedents can be distinguished

Precedents can be overruled

All that is required to turn an easy case into a hard one is to give a normative argument explaining that while a rule is fair and wise in the circumstances in the prior case, it will be harmful or unjust in the case before us. If that argument is plausible—if any reasonable judge would consider it because she is presented with relevant reasons to worry about the fairness or wisdom of rigid application of the rule—the judge will have no choice but to consider the reasons for retaining or rejecting the old rule in these circumstances. That means that a rigid rule cannot be applied mechanically if someone can convince the judge that it should not extend to the case at hand.

Consider the famous case of *Riggs v. Palmer*.[2] A grandfather wrote a will leaving his house and land to his grandson. State statutes empowered owners to write wills to determine who would own their property at death. But the grandson learned that his grandfather was thinking about changing his will. The grandson murdered his grandfather to prevent that from happening. Should the grandson inherit? Rigid application of the statute of wills would say yes; it contained no exception for murder. But, as Justice Cardozo explained in an opinion for the New York Court of Appeals, "it never could have been [the] intention [of the lawmakers] that a donee[3] who murdered the testator[4] to make the will operative should have any benefit under it."[5] The legislature never meant the rule to apply in that instance: "If such a case had been present to their minds, and it had been supposed necessary to make some provision of law to meet it, it cannot be doubted that they would have provided for it."[6] In effect, the court distinguished the statute, determining that it did not apply in the factual circumstances presented by the case at hand. The reasons underlying the rule did not apply because competing, overriding values were at stake.

> A wills statute gives people the right to say who owns their property after they die
>
> But should someone inherit property under a will if they kill the owner to stop him from changing his will?

Because judges can overrule and distinguish cases and because rules do not mechanically determine their own scope, the rigidity, predictability, and mechanical application of rules has no force when a case is hard. Rules are flexible in any hard case where reasons are presented about why the rule should not extend to that case. And when reasons are presented that deserve to be taken seriously, then we are no longer in the world of me-

---

2. 22 N.E. 188, 189 (N.Y. 1889).

3. "Donee" refers to a recipient of a gift or a transfer of property through a will.

4. The "testator" is the one who wrote the will.

5. 22 N.E. at 189.

6. *Id.*

chanical rule application. We are in the world of judgment that character-
izes standards.

§7.3 Why standards are predictable

Just as rules are less predictable than we may have thought, flexible standards are more predictable than we may imagine. Tort law governs every
interaction we have with others, all day every day; it requires us to avoid
negligence and to act reasonably to avoid foreseeable harm to others. Yet
we do not go around all day panicking over each thing we do. In most
instances, that flexible standard is easy to apply. We have cultural and normative knowledge about what kinds of things are and are not "reasonable."
Similarly, the common law of nuisance prohibits substantial, unreasonable
interferences with the use and enjoyment of neighboring land. While this
requires both property owners and judges to make normative judgments to
apply nuisance law, it does not seem to inhibit real estate development or
the enjoyment of property; indeed, it arguably promotes both. Why is that?

Standards comprised of reasonableness tests and multiple factors
achieve shape and substance through the use of explicit or tacit exemplars.

Standards can be predictable
by reference to

– exemplars or stories
– core cases
– situation sense

In the nuisance context, the core case is pollution. The quintessential nuisance case involves
a factory spewing smoke onto neighboring
property, creating conditions that are uncom-
fortable and unhealthful. Conversely, it is not
a nuisance to put up a sign on your front lawn
supporting Barack Obama for President, no
matter how much the neighbors may disagree with the sentiment. Nor is it
a nuisance to paint one's house bright orange.

Nuisance law achieves predictability by reference to core cases like these.
The case of pollution tells a story about a particular kind of conduct with a
particular kind of impact. It vividly embodies the qualitative kind of harm
that nuisance law protects against, and it engages our "situation sense."[7]
Standards operate by identifying core cases covered by the standard and
core cases outside it. A large amount of predictability comes from stories

---

7. Todd Rakoff, *The Implied Terms of Contracts: Of 'Default Rules' and 'Situation-Sense,'*
in *Good Faith and Fault in Contract Law* 191, 201–16 (Jack Beatson & Daniel Friedmann
eds., 1995).

that form exemplars that tell us what is inside and what is outside the standard. Cultural knowledge (including the specialized know-how of lawyers) is needed to understand what it is about the core cases that matters. Hard cases require judgment about where they fit on the spectrum.

When a case is hard, it will be hard whether we are trying to apply a rigid rule or a flexible standard. When a case is easy, it will be similarly easy under either type of legal rule. Both rules and standards can achieve both predictability and flexibility and they do so because normative arguments engage our moral intuitions and require us to make reasoned judgments about the scope of rules and the meaning of standards.

CHAPTER 8.

Interpretation

§8.1 Formal & informal sources of expectations

If you want to find out what rights you have as an employee, where would you look? The first place you might look is your written employment contract—if you have one. If you want to find out where the border is between your property and that of your neighbor, you might look at the deeds or the map recorded by the developer who built the homes in the first place. If you want to know whether you have the right to sublet your apartment, you would probably read your lease agreement.

Written contracts and deeds are formal sources of expectations, and we have good reason to rely on them. After all, we agreed to the terms in those written agreements and they form the basis for the rights and duties of both parties. The law imposes duties on us in our interactions with each other, but contractual arrangements are mechanisms for accepting new obligations toward others while getting something we want in return. Reducing our agreements to writing helps clarify what we are agreeing to and minimizes misunderstanding or mistaken impressions.

At the same time, we have many reasonable expectations based on informal sources such as customs of a trade, social norms, longstanding patterns of conduct, and moral values widely accepted in a community. For example, if your lease says the rent is due on the first of every month, what happens if your check arrives three days late? If the landlord accepts the late rent check for six months in a row, you may come to believe that the landlord has no objections to late payments as long as they arrive within three days of the due date.

Suppose the landlord sues to evict you when the seventh month's check arrives on the third of the month. If we look only to the terms of the agreement, the late payment is a breach of contract and, since timing matters in payments of money (late payments deprive the payee of the use of the money and any resulting interest), the courts may decide that the breach is material, meaning that the time when payment is due concerns a central term of the agreement. Breach of a material term in the lease would ordinarily enable the landlord to evict you.

However, since the landlord has accepted late payments for six months in a row, it may appear that the landlord and tenant have informally renegotiated their agreement. It may seem unfair for the landlord to claim that late payment breaches a material term of the agreement when his informal conduct and failure to complain about late payments for six months in a row may have given the tenant the reasonable impression that the landlord is willing to continue to accept payments a few days after the month begins, meaning that the tenant was in substantial compliance with the lease terms even though her payments were late. Because that is so, many courts will not allow eviction under these circumstances. Rather, they require some warning to the tenant that the rules have changed, and that henceforth payments must be made when due under the written agreement, and if not, the tenant can and will be evicted.

The same thing may be true of an employment agreement. Imagine a law professor who is given a job by a law school to begin teaching in the next academic year starting in September. The professor bargains with the dean for time to prepare lectures and teaching materials and asks if she can move into her office and begin the job on June 1 instead of September 1. The dean agrees and arranges for an office. A yearly salary is part of the arrangement with one-twelfth paid out each month. The new professor moves into her office and starts class preparation in June. July 1st comes around and there is no paycheck. The professor asks the dean about it and the dean tells her that her salary starts in September when the academic year begins. The professor is stunned.

"I asked whether I could get an office and start on the job in June and you said yes!" she says.

The dean is perplexed. "I said you could have an office and begin the job, but I never promised to pay you during the summer."

The professor responds, "But doesn't everyone get paid during the summer?"

The dean responds, "Yes of course, but your appointment does not start until September."

The professor asks, "But I bargained to start in June, and you agreed that I could start work then. Did you think I did not expect to be paid after I quit my old job and started here?"

Clearly what we have here is a failure of communication. While the new professor negotiated to start in June rather than September, the parties to the agreement had different understandings of what that meant.

When the professor asked to begin the job in June, she thought that meant she would be paid. She made an oral request: "can I start in June?" The answer was a letter from the dean saying "yes," telling the new professor that she could move into her office and begin working in June. The new professor knew that she would not start teaching until September but that did not mean she would not be working to prepare for her teaching. After all, all law professors work in the summer to prepare for their fall classes and to produce legal scholarship. She thought it was the custom in the employment market that when you start working, they start paying you unless there is a formal agreement establishing an internship period.

It is not clear the same thing is true in teaching agreements in universities. The university custom is that appointments—and salaries—start in September. The dean thought it was the custom of the trade that academic appointments start in September and that salaries do as well, and the dean assumed the new professor was aware of that custom.

Both the professor and the dean had expectations about what their agreement was. They each had ideas of what things they would need to ask for and what things they did not need to ask for. No language formally said whether or not she would be paid during the summer, but nothing in the letter sent to the professor by the dean said she would not be paid over the summer. Interpreting the meaning of the agreement will require not only reading the letter sent by the dean to the professor but looking at the informal expectations they each had and deciding whether they were—or were not—reasonable. Which one of them had an obligation to speak? Whoever that was, the deal is based not just on the bare terms of the letter but the surrounding norms, customs, and expectations.

Similarly, while written deeds determine borders to real estate, many owners build fences or driveways or even buildings that go over those borders. That is because they make a mistake when they translate the numbers on the document into conduct on the ground. This problem is very, very common. Because it is so common, the law developed the doctrine of adverse possession. One who openly occupies land belonging to another for a long time (specified by state statute) becomes the owner of the land. In adverse possession cases, the parties have usually lived informally for many years with a border they both recognize as the line between their properties. At some point, one of them does a survey and realizes that the recorded border in the formal documents diverges from the facts on the ground. Rigid adherence to the border established in the deeds would destabilize existing expectations rather than protect them. Adverse possession law recognizes those informal expectations as justified.

Expectations may be based on formal sources such as written deeds, maps, contracts

Expectations may also be based on informal sources such as oral promises, conversation, custom, longstanding arrangements

Expectations may be enforced by courts if they are reasonable

Many similar property law doctrines are based on protecting the actual expectations of the parties (based on informal arrangements) despite their divergence from formal sources of rights. When we interpret contract and property arrangements, the law relies on both formal written documents and informal conduct to determine what the agreement was, what the reasonable expectations of the parties are, and what obligations they have to each other.

§8.2 Interpreting ambiguous language

We have just seen that sometimes there is a conflict between the written language in a contract and informal expectations based on conduct, oral communications, or social norms. What happens when we disagree about what the written language in a contract means? First, we are likely to debate whether the language is ambiguous or unambiguous, and if it is unambiguous, what it means. Second, if the language is ambiguous, do we interpret the language based solely on the text of the agreement or do we look to extrinsic evidence, such as the conduct of the parties, to help us figure out what the parties meant to agree to when they signed the contract? And if the text is ambiguous, should our focus be on promoting the reasonable expectations of the parties or promoting desirable public policies?

Consider this problem. A law student has signed a yearlong lease beginning September 1 and ending August 31 of the following year. She gets a summer job in another city and asks her landlord for permission to sublet the apartment to her sister who will live there and pay the rent directly to the landlord. The landlord says no. If the landlord has a right to do that, the tenant will have to pay two rents over the summer: the rent in her current apartment and the rent in an apartment in the city where she will be working. If she cannot afford two rents, she may have to turn down the job. Suppose the lease says: "no subletting without the landlord's consent." Does that clause give the landlord the power to refuse to let the tenant sublet at all or does it require the landlord allow her to sublease unless the landlord has a good reason to refuse?

On one hand, the landlord will argue that the language is unambiguous. Subletting is prohibited unless the landlord agrees, period. No language limits the landlord's discretion or requires the landlord to give a good reason for her refusal. The lease could have limited the landlord's discretion, but it did not do so. The courts cannot add new text to the agreement. If the tenant wanted to be able to sublet, she should have bargained for language that said that the "tenant may sublet the apartment, unless the landlord has a commercially reasonable objection."

Is the contractual language ambiguous or unambiguous?

If it is ambiguous should we focus on the text alone or look to extrinsic evidence such as the conduct of the parties?

If it is ambiguous should we focus on the expectations of the parties or promote desirable public policies?

Do we have no obligations or rights that are not clearly expressed in the agreement?

Or should we be able to interpret contractual arrangements and language in light of ordinary expectations?

Does the implied duty of good faith and fair dealing require contracting parties to act reasonably even if the text of the agreement does not say so?

On the other hand, the tenant will argue that the lease language unambiguously allows subletting. If the landlord had intended to prohibit any sublease at all, the agreement could have simply said: "no subletting." That language would have allowed the landlord to change her mind and agree to a sublease; contracting partners are always free to renegotiate their agreements and to waive their right to enforce contract terms. That language would also have given the landlord an absolute right to refuse the sublease. Alternatively, the language could have stated: "subletting allowed at landlord's unfettered discretion." Some leases are in fact written that way to clarify that the landlord has no duties to give a good reason for refusing to allow the sublease.

That means that, if the landlord wanted absolute power to deny subleasing, the language could have stated that intention clearly. Instead, the language suggested that subletting might be available; the only requirement was getting the landlord's consent. Why does that suggest that the landlord must allow subletting unless she has a good reason to refuse? Common law implies a duty of good faith and fair dealing in every contract. Any agreement that gives one of the parties a discretionary power is usually interpreted to require exercise of that discretionary power in a reasonable manner to protect the justified expectations of both parties. In this case, a tenant who helps the landlord out by finding a reasonable replacement tenant capable of paying the rent protects the landlord's interests by ensuring the property will be occupied and that the landlord can get the rent either from the subtenant or the primary tenant.

It does seem odd that the parties will spend a lot of time arguing about whether an agreement is unambiguous. After all, the fact that they are arguing about what it means is pretty good evidence that it is ambiguous. But these debates happen because the parties want to establish a precedent about what particular language means and they want a judicial ruling that contrary interpretations are unreasonable.

Interpreting this lease requires a judgment about the language normally used to write leases, the ways a reasonable person would interpret the language, and the ways courts in the past have interpreted that language. While courts sometimes read contract and property agreement language strictly, presuming no obligations that were not formally included, they also "read terms into the agreement" based on common understandings of particular commercial arrangements. After all, if you had to write every single expectation into the agreement, you would have to bargain for a long time and the contract would be hundreds of pages long. And you still could not anticipate every issue that could arise or every expectation you have. Courts interpret agreements by assuming they include implied duties of good faith and fair dealing because we should be able to rely on normal expectations to interpret market relationships and we should not have to bargain for protections that are based on custom or common understanding.

Assume that the judge finds the language ambiguous. The lease could have given the landlord absolute discretion or it could have required the landlord to act reasonably; instead, the lease failed to include language of either type. If the language is ambiguous, what do we do now?

One possibility is to focus on the will of the parties. What arrangements did they intend to agree to? What result promotes their reasonable expectations? The landlord will say that she intended to have absolute freedom to refuse a sublease while the tenant will argue that she thought she had bargained for a right to sublease that only required her to get the landlord's consent, which she assumed would be forthcoming if she acted reasonably to protect the landlord's commercial interests.

> When the text of an agreement is ambiguous should the court focus on
>
> – promoting the expectations of the parties or
> – promoting public policies of fairness and social welfare?

A second possibility is to accept the fact that the ambiguity cannot be resolved and that the language has a gap that needs to be filled. Whatever the parties' interpretation of the language, and whatever their expectations based on norms, customs, oral statements, or trade practices, the fact is that they did not read the text in the same way and they did not have a complete "meeting of the minds" on this issue. If that is the case, courts may switch from trying to figure out what the parties were thinking and focus instead on public policy considerations, such as which result is fair or which result is better for society.

The landlord may argue that the court should focus on protecting her property rights. First, when owners lease property they keep any rights they have not given away. The landlord did not give up the right to control access to her property beyond granting possession to the tenant for the year; she did not agree to possession by anyone else. Second, protecting the landlord's prerogatives protects her interests in keeping the property safe and secure. This promotes a central norm of the common law of property because it ensures that property can freely be transferred in the marketplace; lawyers call this "promoting the alienability of land." Third, this result is not unfair to tenants who are free to bargain for a right to sublet or even for a nine-month lease.

The tenant will respond by noting that the landlord may have property rights but so does the tenant. Lease arrangements split property rights between landlord and tenant. The tenant owns a present possessory interest called a "term of years" and the landlord owns a future interest called a "reversion" (the right to get the property back after the lease ends) along with contractual rights to rent and protection of the property from harm. If a central policy norm underlying property law is to increase the "alienability of land," then that policy applies both to the landlord's interest and the tenant's interest. While maximizing landlord control may make the landlord's interest easier to transfer, giving the tenant the right to sublet in a reasonable manner makes the tenant's interest easier to transfer.

Allowing the tenant to sublet would arguably be good because it protects the tenant's right to liberty. If the tenant cannot pay two rents over the summer and has to refuse the job offer, then her autonomy has been limited. She is effectively tied to the land like a feudal peasant. Her right to work, her right to travel, and her right to pursue happiness have all been limited, even though the landlord cannot proffer a good reason to restrict her liberty in this way. Consider that we do not force people to work for other people. Even if you promise to accept a job, the courts will not issue an order forcing you to take it and do the work; there is a little thing called the Thirteenth Amendment that gets in the way. Conversely, the landlord should not be able to prevent the tenant from accepting a job elsewhere unless the landlord has a really good reason—something that is not present here.

If the landlord will not let the tenant sublet, society will lose the value of the tenant's services in a job that would benefit both her and her new employer. Moreover, subletting would allow her to receive those benefits without harming the landlord at all. The landlord is legally guaranteed to receive the rent from either the tenant or the subtenant and both are obligated not to damage the property. The landlord should not be free to refuse without a good reason, such as: if the subtenant was unable to pay the rent.

This discussion illustrates the fact that contract interpretation sometimes focuses on discerning the intent of the parties and sometimes on promoting public policy goals unless the parties make clear they want a different outcome. Contract interpretation is not simply a matter of reading written agreements and doing what they say. It requires understanding and shaping social relationships to promote both fairness and welfare.

§8.3 Statutes

Just as judges (and citizens) must interpret ambiguous contract agreements, they must interpret statutes that govern their conduct and relationships. Many of the same considerations that apply to contract interpretation apply to statutory interpretation as well. The first focus of statutory interpretation is the text of the statute. What do the words say and what do they mean? A second focus is the purpose of the statute, the problems it was intended to address, and the policies it was intended to enact. While some legal scholars and judges argue that we should focus on text alone, other participants in the legal system recognize that the context in which a statute was passed and the explicit or implicit goals of the statute can sometimes help resolve ambiguities.

Title II of the 1964 Civil Rights Act requires public accommodations to provide "full and equal enjoyment" of goods and services without regard to race or religion. It applies to "any place of public accommodation, as defined in this section."[1] The text goes on to say that "each of the following establishments ... is a place of public accommodation."[2] That sentence is followed by a short list that includes hotels, restaurants, entertainment and sports facilities, and gas stations. The question is: does the statute prohibit racial discrimination in retail stores?

At first glance, it seems like an easy case. Only a couple of courts have addressed this question and they have held that the answer is "no." The text puts duties on public accommodations "as defined in this section" and then gives a list of the covered entities. Stores are not on the list. Case closed. The statute is unambiguous.

Why is the case harder than that? First, other statutes contain language making crystal clear that the lists they contain are exhaustive. On one hand, it seems inappropriate to read the word "stores" into the statute when it is not there. On the other hand, if the legislature wanted to clearly state that the list was exhaustive rather than illustrative, it could have done so. This could be done through a definition section or by saying "the following, and only the following" or similar language. Instead, the statute merely says: "each of the following is a place of public accommodation." It is true that the

---

1. 42 U.S.C. §2000a(a).
2. 42 U.S.C. §2000a(b).

statute uses the limiting words "as defined in this section" but that could be simply to differentiate this statute from other federal laws that grant access to businesses open to the public—like the Civil Rights Act of 1866[3]—which may have a different scope.

Second, there may be a reason for the list to be there, other than the desire to make the list exhaustive: these places were where the problem of discrimination was most severe and pervasive. The list could have been meant to emphasize that Congress indeed intended to cover these entities and to make sure that everyone understood that Congress viewed the listed entities as public rather than private in nature. If retail stores generally provided equal access before the law was passed, Congress may have intended to extend that access to the listed establishments where it had historically been denied. In other words, the statute might have been intended to *expand* access to the existing marketplace rather than to *contract* it.

Third, Congress might have deliberately made the statute vague because that was the best way to get the statute passed. Congress could easily have included language answering the question of whether the list was exclusive or illustrative. Perhaps it did not because Congress could neither agree on a longer list, nor agree to make the list exclusive. After all, legislation is a function of compromise among the many members of Congress. Perhaps only vague language could garner majority votes in Congress. Useful ambiguity in statutory language gives courts the job of answering questions that are too politically controversial to resolve in the legislature. Whether or not we think Congress should do this, the fact is that Congress often does exactly this.

When a civil rights law does not clarify whether a list is exclusive or illustrative, how should judges read it? Should courts read civil rights statutes narrowly or broadly? Congress is free to overrule judges, no matter which way they rule, simply by passing a statute. At the same time, it is difficult for legislation to be passed, so whatever the courts say the statute means may be what the law is for the foreseeable future.

We have conflicting canons of interpretation. One canon tells us to defer to the text when it is clear. We have just seen that this does not always definitively answer a question, since each side would argue that the text has a clear meaning but they disagree about what that supposedly clear meaning is. One side would argue that the existence of a list means that those busi-

---

3. 42 U.S.C. §§1981–1982.

nesses, and only those businesses, are covered. The other side will note that the failure to include limiting language means that the category of "public accommodation" is not limited to the listed facilities.

A second canon of interpretation tells us to read "remedial" statutes liberally to effectuate their purposes.[4] If the Civil Rights Act of 1964 was passed to promote equal access to the marketplace, then we should err on the side of promoting that goal. Some judges determine the purposes of statutes by focusing on the intent of the legislature. Given the difficulty of ascribing "intent" to a multimember body, a more useful inquiry is to think about the social and political context in which the statute was passed, the social problem it was intended to solve, and the policies the statute was intended to further. The purpose of this statute was to ensure that people have access to businesses open to the public without regard to race or religion. Reading the statute broadly to encompass all places of public accommodation would accomplish that purpose. If Congress intended to allow racial and religious discrimination in retail stores, it could easily have said so; because it did not, we would need good reason to believe that Congress wanted discrimination in retail stores to continue while prohibiting it in hotels, restaurants, and places of entertainment. There is no evidence of that sort and thus no reason to read the statute narrowly.

Of course, a counterargument is that Congress often addresses one problem at a time. Perhaps Congress was able to agree to regulate a short list of places, but it could not agree on a wider list, and the proponents of the law thought that half a loaf was better than nothing at all. In interpreting a statute, the courts should enforce the law that Congress passed, not the law we wish Congress had passed.

Fourth, if the statute is ambiguous, should we focus on the Congress that passed the Civil Rights Act of 1964 or should we also take into account the evolution of federal antidiscrimination statutes passed since 1964? The traditional focus is on the intent of the legislature that passed the law back in 1964. However, if later statutes expanded civil rights protections, that may mean that the current Congress wants broad protection for civil rights and would be happy with a broad interpretation of an ambiguous older statute. That would render the older statute consistent with evolving legislation. Interpreting statutes in light of current legislative policy may be a better

---

4. In the context of this canon of interpretation "remedial laws" are those passed to solve a social problem or to remedy a wrong.

way to defer to legislative intent than focusing on the original intent of the Congress that passed the statute we are interpreting.

The most recent federal public accommodations law is the 1990 Americans with Disabilities Act (the ADA).[5] That statute has a long list of public accommodations, and it includes retail stores along with doctors' and lawyers' offices, universities, and insurance companies.[6] The ADA is our best evidence of our society's current understanding of what a public accommodation is; it embodies common perceptions and expectations, and it enacts contemporary legislative views on the question. If you ask someone on the street whether it is lawful to discriminate on the basis of race in a retail store, they would be surprised to hear that it is lawful. Because of that, perhaps we should interpret ambiguous statutory terms in ways that cohere with current legislative, political, and social values.

If stores are not covered under federal antidiscrimination law, then the only remedy for racial discrimination in retail stores would be under state law. Most states have such laws. But five states do not. They are Alabama, Georgia, Mississippi, South Carolina, and Texas. If no federal law prohibits racial discrimination in retail stores, then racial discrimination in retail stores is not prohibited in those states. However, racial discrimination in retail stores is inconsistent with our evolving legal tradition, as well as with the fundamental values of liberty and equality in a free and democratic society. Moreover, if a court held that retail stores may not discriminate on the basis of race, how likely is it that the current Congress would overrule that decision? The answer is: highly unlikely. The reverse, however, is not true. If a court ruled that racial discrimination is permitted in retail stores, there would be a countermovement to amend the 1964 Civil Rights Act to prohibit such discrimination, and Congress would at least be receptive to it. Reading the statute broadly is arguably more deferential to the legislature than making a ruling that will be publicly decried as contrary to settled legal principles and American values.

This statutory interpretation case started out looking easy: stores are not listed in the 1964 Civil Rights Act and so are not subject to its requirement of equal access. The issue became hard when we focused on (a) what is at

---

5. 42 U.S.C. §12102 *et seq.*
6. 42 U.S.C. §12181(7).

stake; (b) the lessons of history; (c) settled and evolving legislative policy; and (d) norms and values.

§8.4 Constitutions

Some scholars and judges think that the way to interpret ambiguous constitutional provisions is to focus on the meaning of the text alone. We can figure that out by consulting a dictionary. Others argue that we should focus on the original intent of those who drafted the Constitution. Still others think that both the text of the Constitution and original intent are ambiguous and thus cannot tell us what to do in contested cases, especially ones involving issues that were not on the radar screen in 1789 or 1868. They argue that we should understand the Constitution as comprising an evolving tradition.

If we are interested in original intent, what level of generality do we use? The equal protection clause of the fourteenth amendment was interpreted in the twentieth century to prohibit laws that discriminate on the basis of sex even though no one thinks that was the original intent of the amendment, which focused on race. Do we look to the fact that the voters who approved the amendment in 1868 likely favored sex discrimination but opposed race discrimination, or do we focus on the fact that they adopted a general right to equal treatment and that the meaning of equality has been reinterpreted over time? The need to address these ambiguities is what justifies the view of the Constitution as an evolving tradition that affirms our fundamental values and codifies them by identifying fundamental rights that protect us from oppressive laws or actions by government officials.

> When the text of the Constitution is ambiguous should we:
>
> Try to discern the original intent of the framers?
>
> Or promote evolving norms of liberty and equality and democracy?

There is no question that constitutional rights have in fact evolved over time as our social conditions and values have changed. Legally mandated racial segregation held lawful in 1897 in *Plessy v. Ferguson*[7] was held to violate the fourteenth amendment in 1954 in *Brown v. Board of Education*.[8]

---

7. 163 U.S. 537 (1896)
8. 347 U.S. 483 (1954).

Minimum wage laws that were held to be unconstitutional deprivations of liberty in the 1923 case of *Adkins v. Children's Hospital*[9] were held to be valid exercises of Congress's power to legislate to promote the general welfare in 1937 in *West Coast Hotel v. Parrish*.[10] A federal statute prohibiting racial discrimination in public accommodations was struck down as unconstitutional in 1883 in *The Civil Rights Cases*[11] because it regulated private conduct rather than state action while a very similar law was upheld in 1964 in *Heart of Atlanta Motel, Inc. v. United States*[12] as a rational regulation of interstate commerce. Prohibitions on same-sex marriage deemed constitutional in 1972 in *Baker v. Nelson*[13] were held unconstitutional in 2015 in *Obergefell v. Hodges*.[14]

Constitutional interpretation inevitably involves value judgments and normative argument. Consider the case of *Shelley v. Kraemer*.[15] Neighbors on a street in Saint Louis entered into an agreement by which they promised not to allow their homes to be sold to, or occupied by, anyone who was of African American or of Asian ancestry. One owner defied that agreement and sold his home to the Shelleys, an African American family. The state courts in Missouri held that court enforcement of the racially restrictive covenant would not deprive the Shelleys of equal protection of law. Those state courts argued that the agreement was between private parties and the fourteenth amendment's equal protection clause was designed to prevent states from denying equal rights; it said nothing about private conduct. If the equal protection norm applied to private conduct, then you might lose the freedom to decide who to invite to your house for dinner.

The Supreme Court reversed the ruling of the Missouri Supreme Court. It held that court enforcement of racist deed restrictions constituted "state action" that denies access to property on account of race.[16] If the Court had agreed with the Missouri Supreme Court and enforced the covenant, then the sheriff might have had to come and forcibly remove the Shelley

---

9. 261 U.S. 525 (1923).
10. 300 U.S. 379 (1937).
11. 109 U.S. 3 (1883).
12. 379 U.S. 241 (1964).
13. 409 U.S. 810 (1972).
14. 135 S.Ct. 2584 (2015).
15. 334 U.S. 1 (1948).
16. *Id.*

family from their home. It would seem that that would constitute state involvement in preventing people from acquiring property solely because of their race. Enforcement of those restrictions would help perpetuate racial segregation and would limit access to the housing market in a racially exclusionary manner.

Shelley is thought to be a hard case because it would seem to make every contract enforcement dispute and every trespass suit into a federal case. Where do we draw the line between state action and private action? On one hand, we want to reserve a large area of autonomy where people are free to choose with whom to associate and how to live their lives. Forcing people to treat every other person "equally" would be both impossible and absurd; it would prevent us from having friends, for example.

On the other hand, there is no doubt that many white people turned to using racial covenants to keep African Americans out of their neighborhoods after the Supreme Court held in 1917 that cities could not enact zoning laws that segregated housing by race.[17] If the Supreme Court had affirmed the Missouri Supreme Court's opinion in *Shelley v. Kraemer*, it would have put the state firmly on the side of promoting—and enforcing—racial discrimination in housing. Since the Court was confronted with an either/or choice—enforce private racial covenants or refuse to enforce them—it had no choice but to take sides in a politically controversial issue.[18]

Constitutional interpretation requires normative argument about our most fundamental values. It is one way we define the human rights that should be protected from infringement by the state and by which we protect people from oppression. That is true whether we focus on the text of the Constitution, the original intent of the framers, or our evolving norms of justice and fairness.

---

17. Buchanan v. Warley, 245 U.S. 60 (1917).

18. For a history of the many ways the U.S. government promoted racial segregation in the housing market, *see* Richard Rothstein, *The Color of Law: A Forgotten History of How Our Government Segregated America* (2017).

SUMMARY OF RULE OF LAW ARGUMENTS

CASES & RULES

Precedent

- ☑ Apply precedent
- ☑ Distinguish precedent
- ☑ Reconcile conflicting precedents
- ☑ Overrule precedent

Rules & Standards

Rigid rules are predictable	Flexible standards allow justice in individual case
Rules are flexible	Standards are predictable

Interpretation

Formal, written sources alone to create legitimate expectations	Informal sources of expectation matter
Text is unambiguous	Text is ambiguous
If ambiguous, promote the will of the parties	If ambiguous, promote public policy

Democracy & the Rule of Law

Judicial restraint	Judicial activism
Defer to legislature to change the law	Modernize common law to accord with current legislation and evolving values
Legislative competence	Judicial competence

PART 4.

Justifications

CHAPTER 9.

Framing

§9.1 Justification and the "because" clause

Once a decision maker has heard the best arguments on both sides, what happens then? How does a judge decide which way to go and what reasons can the judge give to justify why she accepted one set of arguments over the other set? That is the role of justification—the art of giving reasons to explain why one value should prevail over another or one interpretation of a value should be adopted over another interpretation. Judges cannot simply choose one side or the other and say: "I'm with you." If they cannot provide justifications for the result, their choices will seem—and may well be—arbitrary. We will have no sense that they are treating like cases alike. Nor will we have any confidence that they have done the right thing. We need a way of completing this thought: "Although sometimes freedom of action should be protected even if it harms the security of others, this case is one where people should be free from this kind of harm. That is because..." What do we say after that? How do we finish the "because" clause?

Lawyers and judges use various techniques to explain why one argument should prevail over another. Some of these techniques use standard arguments but elevate them so that they provide justifications for choosing one argument over a counterargument in the context presented by the case. Other techniques seek to step over the arguments to develop an impartial point of view that can help us judge how to resolve a clash of competing values or arguments. Three approaches to justification are typical in judicial decisions: (1) framing, (2) value specification and contextualization, and (3) prioritization.

The first way we can justify a legal rule or result is by framing the issue so we can understand what the problem is about. We do that (a) by articulating our background assumptions; (b) by framing the question; and (c) by telling the story. These ways of orienting ourselves are crucial in helping see why one set of arguments should prevail over another.

The second technique is to specify the meaning of values and identify the social contexts in which they apply. We can do that by (a) articulating our sense of the situation; (b) defining the appropriate contexts within which values can be legitimately asserted; and (c) attending to historical changes in values and conditions. In effect, we make the problem go away by restrained interpretation of values, i.e., explanations of when values are and are not relevant to human relationships. Narrowing the legitimate scope of application of values to appropriate situations may render values consistent with each other even though, at a more abstract level, they initially seemed to contradict each other.

Third, when it is not possible to render competing values consistent with each other by delineating the social contexts within which they are appropriately expressed, we must figure out a way to prioritize one set of interests, rights, or values over another set in the case at hand. Our goal is to generate reasons that could be accepted by the losing side. We can do this (a) by balancing interests; (b) by Golden Rule reasoning that asks if we could accept a result if we were on the other side or by asking what rule we would adopt if we had to sign a social contract that could obtain universal agreement; and (c) reflective equilibrium, or reasoning back and forth between values and principles on one hand and specific cases on the other, to develop a reasonable way to reconcile and draw lines between competing interests and rights and to present a coherent set of justifications for the lines we are drawing between rules and among cases.

This chapter, and those that follow, explain these methods of justification and give examples of how to use them. To help us understand these justificatory techniques, consider the hypo described in the following section.

§9.2 A hypo: flying the American flag

Shortly after 9/11, Justice Clarence Thomas's father-in-law, Donald Lamp, placed an American flag on his condominium balcony.[1] The condominium association asked him to take it down. The flag violated a rule adopted by the association that prohibited any external decorations on the condo units. No flags, no banners, no wind chimes, no political signs. But emotions ran strong at that time, and Lamp refused to take down his flag. Eventually, the association gave in and waived its right to enforce its rule.

If the association had insisted on enforcing its rule and had sued Lamp in court asking the judge to order Lamp to take down the flag, who should win that lawsuit? State statutes empower owners to create condominium complexes that divide property rights among the owners. Unit owners own the space inside their condo apartments, and they own in common the areas they share, such as hallways, roofs, external walls, and facilities inside the walls. Those common areas are managed by the condominium association and the management board selected by the owners. Condo associations have the power to enact rules governing use and appearance of common areas (including external walls and balconies) and some types of activity inside apartments that affect others, as long as those rules are reasonable. Was the rule against flags on the balconies reasonable in the context of this case?

> Condominium associations have the power to enforce rules as long as they are reasonable

There are rights arguments on both sides. Lamp is the owner of his condo and he claims a right of freedom of action to do what he likes with his own property as long as it does not harm others. One of my students put it this way: "An American wants to fly the American flag from the balcony of his home after the United States is attacked by foreign enemies and you want the sheriff to come to force him to take it down? That's not liberty; that's oppression." Condo associations have the power to enact rules, but those rules must be reasonable. Rules cannot intrude on fundamental rights of owners, and those rights include freedom of speech. Lamp's freedom to

---

1. Associated Press, *Apartment dweller, managers clash over flag display*, June 6, 2004, http://www.firstamendmentcenter.org/news.aspx?id=13469; *see also* Tony Mauro, *An unwelcome mat for free speech*, USA Today, Aug. 18, 2004, at 13A; Eric Olson, *Father-in-Law of High Court Justice Defies Rule, Flies Flag*, St. Louis Post-Dispatch, May 29, 2004, at 6.

express his solidarity with the nation after it has been attacked by terrorists is a powerful and legitimate interest.

On the other side, the association claims a right of security in enforcement of rules validly promulgated by the association through voting procedures that created the association and its management board. Flags affect the external appearance of the building in a way that the majority of owners deem unsightly, especially if every owner were allowed to place flags or decorations of any kind on the outside of the building. By buying a condominium unit, Lamp agreed to abide by rules of the association; in so doing, he limited his own freedom. He simply does not own the right to fly the flag on the balcony. If he wanted to reserve such a right, he should have bought a single-family home not subject to a homeowners association or he could have tried to get the association to change the rules. The association is free to adopt rules that serve the owners' interests and it has a right to enforce those rules. Freedom of contract gave the rights of the majority the power to promulgate the rule, and, because Lamp promised to abide by such rules, he has a duty to comply.

There are costs and benefits of the alternative rules. Allowing condo owners to defy validly enacted rules will mean that neighbors will never be sure whether they can collectively make and enforce rules that benefit everyone in the building. Anything they do could be second-guessed by a court. If they cannot control their environment, the market value of the units could be reduced while interfering with the owners' use and enjoyment of their homes. The benefits of enforcing covenants about aesthetic appearance of the building arguably outweigh any costs, especially when the unit owners contractually agreed to be bound by rules passed by the majority of owners. Lamp could have avoided the costs of compliance with the rule by buying a home not subject to regulation by a homeowners association.

The market will discipline the association if it adopts unreasonable rules. If a rule against flying the American flag makes the condo units less attractive on the real estate market, then their value will decrease. If it turns out that the fair market value of the units goes down after the rule is put in place, or if owners have trouble selling their units, that may give the association the incentive to repeal the rule. If it does not repeal the rule, that suggests that, to them, the benefits of the rule outweigh its costs. There is no need for regulation to change the result; market forces will ensure that the benefits of condo rules exceed their costs.

Unit owner Lamp will respond that he has no objection to enforcing most rules about use or appearance of common areas. But the benefits of a rule preventing the flying of the American flag are outweighed by its costs. We are not talking only about market value of the apartment but a restraint of a fundamental right. The rule impinges on core property rights and liberties. Such a rule, if adopted generally, would affect the millions of Americans who live in housing governed by homeowners associations. If there is no limit on the rules that such associations can promulgate, then neighbors will be empowered to interfere with personal decisions that owners make about how to use their own property with a consequent loss of the ability to live freely in their own homes. The law should protect minority owners from oppressive rules promulgated by the majority. When an association rule violates fundamental rights embodied in the First Amendment, depriving the owner of the right of free speech, then giving neighbors the freedom to strip an owner of those rights imposes costs that outweigh any benefits.

Assume these arguments form the platform from which we will decide the case. Assume also that the arguments on both sides are plausible and relevant; they are things we should consider in making a decision. So now how can we justify a rule choice here in a way that shows respect for both sides? How can we give reasons to adopt one set of arguments over the other? Is it possible to explain the result in a way that could potentially be persuasive to the losing party?

The set of justification techniques discussed in this chapter focuses on ways we can provide a frame of reference for what the case is about, what the choice means, and what is at stake. Three ways to do this are (a) making explicit the background understandings we have about the problem; (b) framing the issue we need to address; and (c) telling the story in a way that is evocative and prompts appropriate emotional responses to the case.

§9.3 Background understandings

The first step in normative decision making is to orient ourselves in a moral universe. We have both conscious and unconscious assumptions about what the world is like and what it should be like. In debate about the right way to deal with a dispute, we often find competing orientations, including different assumptions about human nature, the good society, social relationships, the right way to think about justice, and the right way to view the facts. Philosopher Charles Taylor has called these fundamental assumptions "social imaginaries" or "background pictures" that inform and frame our conceptions of social life and human relationships.[2] Importantly for law, background understandings shape our conceptions of the legal framework of a free and democratic society. In making a persuasive argument, it helps to be aware of competing background assumptions. We also gain traction by articulating those assumptions so that we can be more reflective about their validity or defensibility.

Henry Richardson explains that "[w]hen people differ radically over what they take to be axiomatic, it is likely that they also arrived at these beliefs through strikingly different tacit exemplars."[3] Exemplars are analogies that frame our understanding of what a case is about, what moral and practical issues are implicated in it, who is the hero and who is the villain in the story. These exemplars may be tacit because we may not be aware that we are choosing one way of seeing an issue rather than another.

For example, the owner in our flag case focuses on the fact that he owns his condo. No one else has the right to be on his balcony. And while it is true that the deed to his property subjects him to reasonable rules promulgated by the association, it has no right to tell him what to do inside his own home. From his standpoint, while the association may be in charge of re-pointing the bricks on the outside of the building or painting the trim, that does not mean it can tell him what to do on his own balcony.

An owner's rights in his own home?

Or the property rights of the neighbors who seek a home environment they cherish?

The association sees the case very differently. The association has the power to regulate the external appearance of the building and was created precisely because the owners care about the environment within which their homes are located. They got together to ensure that the homes they were buying would be in a neighborhood context they find peaceful, beautiful, comforting. Lamp benefits from that environment as much as his neighbors do, and he agreed to abide by the environmental rules. He may have freedom of conduct within his own house, but he does not own the right to defy rules about decorations visible on the outside of the building. The people who own that right are his neighbors, the members of the association that agreed to

2. Charles Taylor, *Modern Social Imaginaries* 3–4, 8, 23 (2004).
3. Henry S. Richardson, *Practical Reasoning About Final Ends* 271 (1997).

the rules prohibiting flags and other decorations on the balconies. The association is not infringing on the owner's property rights; by defying a rule adopted by the majority, he is infringing on their shared property rights in common areas.

The owner will also frame the case as one involving the fundamental right of freedom of speech. He should be able to express himself by flying the American flag after the country is attacked by foreign enemies. The association will respond that his freedom of speech does not give him the right to enter the apartments of his neighbors and lecture them on his political views. His free speech rights cannot be exercised on someone else's property. Because the external walls are within the jurisdiction of the association and are commonly owned, he is not entitled to use those areas in violation of validly enacted rules, even if he is doing so for speech purposes.

Freedom of speech?

Or trespass on the property rights of others?

We have a contest of background understandings and tacit exemplars. Making a persuasive argument on one side or the other may require bringing these background pictures to light and giving reasons why one way of looking at the dispute is more apt and appropriate than the other. Doing so engages our moral intuitions about the social context and helps us to provide reasons that can complete the "because" clause.

§9.4 Framing the issue

Lawyers begin their arguments in written briefs by stating the question presented by the case. For example, while the unit owner may ask: "Do owners have the right to exercise free speech on their own property?" the association may ask a very different question: "why should one owner be free to violate rules that benefit everyone and that he agreed to?"

Arguments are won and lost by the way the litigants frame the question. Framing the question can place the burden on the other side to justify what they want to happen. Framing an issue often focuses attention on particular values and asks why the other party can claim a right to violate them. The goal is to ask a question that

Frame the issue so the question seems to answer itself

Try to place the burden on the other side to justify infringing on important rights or interests

Switch from rights to interests to suggest alternative ways to promote the other side's goals seems to answer itself. Asking whether I have the right to control my own house suggests that the owner's actions are self-regarding. Why should others care what I do in my own home? Why don't they just leave me alone? Asking why the owner should be free to flout rules that benefit everyone and that he agreed to follow suggests that the owner (not the association) is the one violating the property rights of others.

Another way to frame the question is to focus on interests underlying rights, and then to suggest alternative ways to satisfy those interests. The owner has a strong interest in expressing himself, but aren't there ways to do this other than by flying the flag in defiance of a rule he agreed to abide by? Conversely, can't the association's interest in a uniform external appearance of the building be sufficiently promoted even if an exception is made for the American flag, given its unique role in American life? The goal of framing the question is to reverse the polarity of who has the burden of proof on the question. Doing this can highlight a particular conception of the relevance and relative strength of the competing values in the case.

When the two sides present alternative ways of framing the issue, this helps the decision maker gain a deeper understanding of what is at stake. Arguments supplement issue framing and they can help persuade the decision maker that one way of framing the issue is more appropriate than other ways.

§9.5 Storytelling

In addition to making background assumptions explicit and framing the question, a third way that lawyers engage in framing our understanding of the case is through storytelling. Every judicial opinion starts with a recitation of the facts. The facts form a narrative and that helps us see the moral of the story. Lawyers create a core theory of the dispute that they want the judge to understand; constructing a story from the facts is a crucial part of this task. Coming to see the case one way or another is part of how lawyers, judges, and jurors decide what the case means. Storytelling is part of the way we reason about moral questions. It engages our moral sympathy. Stories help us come to see what matters and why.

The owner may tell the story by focusing on the specific facts that gave rise to the dispute: the United States suffered its worst attack by foreign enemies since Pearl Harbor. The country was struck with grief and anger

and outrage. Lamb wanted to express his love of the country and his solidarity with all Americans. Flying the
flag hurt no one. It did not, and could
not, lower the fair market value of the
property. He did not paint his balcony
purple. He did not blare loud music. All
he did was what millions of other Americans did. What possibly could justify
stopping him from joining them in
showing his love of the country and
grief at unspeakable human loss?

> Stories focus on the facts to help us see what they mean
>
> Stories identify victims and villains
>
> Stories engage our moral sympathies and emotional responses
>
> Stories help us engage in moral reasoning

The association is likely to start the story much earlier. We are talking about a condominium building. The owner had a choice of buying a single-family home or a condo or renting. He had a choice of where to live, knowing that different towns have different zoning laws and that different subdivisions have different homeowners associations with different rules. If he wanted a place free from such rules, he should have looked for it. Instead, he agreed to buy housing that was regulated by rules and he benefited from them. He cannot complain that he does not want to abide by the very rules that made his apartment attractive in the first place. Nor can he benefit from the rules while breaking them himself.

These alternative stories try to make the listener sympathetic to the situation of the party making the argument. They shape our understanding of who is, and who is not, acting reasonably. They shift images of victims and villains and they give alternative pictures of what the case is about. They help us choose between competing sets of arguments because they invite us to see the case in different ways. Decision makers who must give reasons for going one way or another can justify their decisions partly by telling the story in a way that frames our understanding of the relative strength of competing interests and the pertinence of competing rights claims.

CHAPTER 10

Value Specification & Contextualization

§10.1 Specifying the meaning of values

Hard cases either require us to choose between alternative conceptions of a common value or between competing values. When we face choices like that, we need to take another step. We must specify what values mean in concrete terms and we must identify the contexts in which those values reasonably apply. Abraham Lincoln explained this in a speech given in 1864:

> The world has never had a good definition of the word liberty. And the American people just now are much in want of one. We all declare for liberty; but in using the same *word* we do not mean the same *thing*. With some, the word liberty may mean for each man to do as he pleases with himself and the product of his labor; while with others the same word may mean for some men to do as they please with other men, and the product of other men's labor. Here are two, not only different, but incompatible things, called by the same name, liberty. And it follows that each of the things is by the respective parties called by two different and incompatible names, liberty and tyranny.[1]

---

1. Abraham Lincoln, *Address at the Sanitary Fair* (Baltimore, Apr. 18, 1864), reprinted in *Abraham Lincoln: His Speeches and Writings* 748–49 (R. Basler ed. 1946).

One might not have thought that those arguing for the institution of slavery might use the idea of liberty to justify it, but that is because times have changed so much that we cannot easily see how the cause of slavery could be linked in someone's mind with the value of liberty. When we recall that enslaved persons were deemed to be a species of "property" and that one aspect of liberty may be the freedom to acquire and use property, we can see that the dispute over slavery is an argument about the legitimacy of asserting property rights in human beings. That, in turn, requires specification of the meaning and scope of the concept of liberty. Abraham Lincoln understood that one way to justify a choice is to specify what a value really means.

When we face conflicting value claims, one way to resolve the conflict is to reinterpret those values so that the conflict disappears. In the slavery context, the conflict disappears once we understand that there is no conceivable justification for allowing people to own other people; that is not a liberty at all. In that case, the value conflict disappears; only one side has a case at all. The same thing may occur when we have conflicting values. Conflicts can sometimes be resolved if we define competing values in a manner that makes them consistent with each other. We may be able to do that by specifying what the values mean or by defining the social contexts to which they legitimately apply. If we can narrow the scope of one or both values, they may not conflict at all.

Concepts are general (like "liberty") Conceptions are specifications of concepts (like "free use of one's own property")

When a case involves competing interpretations of a particular value, we need to specify what that value means in order to determine whether it applies to the case we are trying to resolve. In our American flag case, both the condo association and the unit owner may base their claims on their right to liberty. But they mean different things when they appeal to that value. Does "liberty" refer to the freedom to control one's own property or the freedom to contract with others to create a governing entity with the power to adopt aesthetic controls for common areas? The general concept of liberty must be converted to a more specific conceptualization that defines its precise meaning.

The owner may also define liberty as the right to fly the American flag in front of his own home. In the face of an enemy attack, he felt the need to do something to show others that he stands with the victims, that he respects and grieves with them, that he is resolute in standing up for our nation and its right to protect itself from attack. The American flag is a symbol of national unity. The liberty claim he is making is a narrow one. He is not asking to be able to decorate his part of the external wall in a way that would mar its appearance. He is not asking for a right to paint his balcony purple, play loud music outside, post political ads, or use a bullhorn to make speeches from his balcony. He is only asking for the right to fly the American flag in a time of crisis. If he specifies the value he is asking for by limiting his claim in this manner, he may be able to convince the decision maker that protecting his interest will not harm the interests or rights of others or impinge on competing values asserted by the association. At the same time, he may more easily convince the decision maker that the value of liberty is a valid justification for making an exception to otherwise-applicable condo rules.

> Autonomy; freedom to show one's love of country; power to control one's own property and private space
>
> Property rights of neighbors; freedom of contract; obligation to abide by one's promises

The association will acknowledge the heartfelt impulses expressed by the unit owner. He is right to feel all that; he is right to love the country; he is entitled to express himself. But he is not entitled to exercise his right to freedom of speech in a way that tramples on the property rights of others. He has a right to liberty, but so do his neighbors. He owns his unit, but he does not own the external walls of the building; those walls are owned collectively by all the unit owners in the building. The condo association is the entity that has the right to make decisions about the external appearance of the building. If that is so, then the unit owner has no legitimate liberty claim here at all. If liberty is implicated in this case, it is the liberty of owners to manage commonly-owned property by majority rule.

Value specification can justify results in contested cases by explaining why a value is—or is not—implicated in a particular fact situation. Lamp claims a right to fly the American flag; at the same time, he is asserting that the association has no right to stop him from doing that. The association claims a right to regulate the external walls of the building and that Lamp has no right to ignore the rules it adopts. Each side is asserting a value but each side is also claiming that the other side has no legitimate claim at all. The association says that there is no such thing as a liberty interest in violating condo rules; the unit owner says there is no such thing as a liberty interest in preventing someone from flying the American flag in front of his home. In effect, they are each arguing that the other side misunderstands the meaning of "liberty." One way to justify a ruling in a contested case is to explain which side is right when they present conflicting interpretations of the same value.

§10.2 Social context & restrained interpretation of values

When both sides have identified relevant values or plausible competing interpretations of a single value, we need a way to justify the decision while recognizing that both sides have plausible value claims. Is there a way to recognize competing values while making the conflict between them disappear? The answer is yes if we can reinterpret the competing values to render them consistent with each other. Values that appear to conflict may be seen to be consistent if we can distinguish the social contexts in which they each apply.

For example, property owners generally have freedom to exclude others from their property, but that does not mean they have the right to exclude people from public accommodations because of their race or religion. The right to exclude promotes the values of autonomy, security, privacy, freedom of association, and freedom of religion, among others. When we are talking about homes or religious institutions or private associations, those values are relevant and generally outweigh competing values. But public accommodations play a particular function in our economic, social, and political system. They enable people to enter the marketplace to purchase goods and services without needing to call ahead or check to see if the store serves people like them. Prohibiting invidious discrimination in public accommodations promotes equal access to the marketplace without regard to race, religion, or other factors that should not prevent equal participation in social and economic life. That distinguishes public accommodations from homes or religious institutions.

This suggests that we may be able to adjudicate value conflicts by restrained interpretation of values. If one value holds sway in one social context while a different value holds sway in another social context, we may conclude that the values do not conflict at all but are actually consistent with each other. Freedom of association is arguably pertinent in spheres of social life where choices about association should be protected (the home, the religious institution, friendship, political association) but it is not pertinent in spheres of social life to which the norm of equal access should apply (public accommodations, employment, housing), at least when we are talking about invidious discrimination that legislatures have chosen to ban from the marketplace. Those public spheres of the marketplace are governed by the value of promoting equal access not freedom of association. By defining the appropriate social contexts in which values are relevant, we may be able to justify a decision by restrained interpretation of one value or another so that they do not actually conflict at all.

Restrained interpretation of a value acknowledges its power generally but denies its pertinence or relevance in a specific social context

Narrowing the scope of application of the value may render it consistent with competing values rather than in tension with them

The owner in our flag-flying case may argue that the American flag is different from other symbols. While the association has liberty interests in managing common areas, that liberty does not extend to limitations on flying the American flag in front of one's home, especially after a national tragedy. This is not an ordinary conflict about the reasonableness of a condominium rule; we are talking about the rights of an American to free speech in the days after 9/11. We are talking about the American flag. That context changes everything. On this interpretation, the unit owner has valid liberty interests and the condo association does not.

The association will argue that this case is about the powers that condo associations have to regulate commonly owned areas. If Lamp owned a single-family home with no restrictions in his deed making him subject to rules promulgated by a homeowners association, things would be different and he would be free to fly the American flag. But the condominium context is different. As one court noted, "condominium living is unique and involves a greater degree of restrictions on the rights of the individual unit owners when compared to other property owners."[2] The condominium context entails common areas that are legitimately subject to regulation by the majority of owners. The liberty interests at stake here are those of the condo association, not the unit owner who seeks to violate valid rules designed to protect common property rights. On this interpretation, the condo association has valid liberty interests and the unit owner does not.

---

2. Woodside Village Condominium Ass'n, Inc. v. Jahren, 806 So. 2d 452, 456 (Fla. 2002)

CHAPTER 11

Prioritization

§11.1 Balancing interests

In the last chapter we focused on ways to make value conflicts disappear by rendering values consistent with each other. What if that doesn't work? We need a way to solve an intractable value conflict by explaining why one value should prevail over another or be given priority when they conflict. The most common way lawyers do this is by balancing interests. We may say that one value outweighs the other in the context of this case. That requires an analysis of the relative strength or weight of the competing interests given the dispute before us. Balancing language admits that conflicting values command our allegiance at the same time while pulling us in different directions. We then assert that one set of interests should prevail over the other set because, on balance, that is the right choice to make.

In our flag-flying case, the owner will argue that his right to freedom of speech should prevail over mere aesthetic concerns. The harm from stopping him from flying the flag is great; the harm from allowing him to fly it is small. While condo associations generally have the right to regulate common areas, that right should give way in the face of fundamental rights. That does not mean that unit owners have the right to festoon their balconies with campaign posters, but it should at least give owners the right to fly the American flag because it is the symbol of our nation.

The association will argue it is not undermining his freedom of speech in any significant way. It is simply stopping him from exercising his rights on someone else's property and in violation of his own contractual commitments. By buying a condo unit subject to condo rules, he agreed to be bound by those rules, and he has no right to renege on his commitments. He has other ways of engaging in speech and showing his solidarity with his fellow Americans so the cost to him of enforcing the rule is small. The converse is not true. The ability of the owners to freely create rules governing common areas will be lost if individual owners were free to defect any time they liked, simply by characterizing their actions as having an expressive component. The benefits of condominium living can only exist because owners are subject to reasonable rules promulgated by the association.

§11.2 The Golden Rule, the social contract & reasons we can accept

A different way to prioritize competing interests, rights, or values is to use some version of the Golden Rule or the social contract. The Golden Rule asks us to empathize with others and ask if we would be demanding the same thing if we were in their place. Social contract reasoning asks us to imagine the rule we would adopt if we were in an initial position setting the rules that would bind, not only other people, but ourselves as well.

Golden Rule reasoning: could we accept the result as fair if we (or those we love) were on the other side of the dispute? (role reversal)

Social contract reasoning: what rules would we adopt if we did not know our position in society or our particular interests?

We begin with the observation that treating others with dignity requires us to try to see the world from their point of view as well as from our own. Christine Korsgaard and T. M. Scanlon have both argued that morality requires that we justify our actions by reasons others can accept or cannot reasonably reject.[1] John Rawls applies this principle to the social contract tradition of Hobbes and Locke by asking what rules of the game we would favor if we did not know in advance

---

1. Christine M. Korsgaard, *The Authority of Reflection*, in *The Sources of Normativity* 90, 113–15 (Onora O'Neill ed. 1996); T.M. Scanlon, *What We Owe to Each Other* (1998).

what role we would play in society. What rules could we unanimously accept if we were designing a framework that would allow free and equal persons to live together in a society with persistent diversity on the meaning of the good life? If we respect each person's dignity and freedom, we must consider what choices reasonable persons would make about the basic structure of society if they could not be sure that they would be the ones in charge of the government.[2] The method of reversing roles, of defending an outcome to the losing side, of recognizing the costs as well as the benefits of any rule, is a staple of normative argument used by lawyers.

Social contract reasoning is actually a social version of the Golden Rule. The positive version is "treat others as you would want to be treated"; the negative version is "don't do to others what you would not want done to yourself." The so-called "platinum rule" is "do not do unto others what they would not want done to themselves." Each of these formulations requires us to see the problem from the other person's point of view. We cannot justify a ruling one way or the other if we cannot come up with reasons the losing side could accept.

Our flag-flying owner may ask his neighbors to think about the fact that the Supreme Court has held that private property owners have a First Amendment right to post signs on their lawns; that right surely includes the right to fly the American flag.[3] Any local zoning law that completely prohibits signs or flags is unconstitutional. While the First Amendment applies only to state action (like a zoning law) and not to private action (like condo rules), the owner asks why he should be deprived of the same right to fly the flag as is enjoyed by other Americans. While it makes sense to allow condo associations to make rules about common areas, it should not have the power to infringe on fundamental rights like freedom of speech.

The association may argue that the conflict arises here because an owner seeks to secede from a way of life that includes common ownership of common areas. Those areas need to be governed and democracy requires the consent of the governed for legitimate rules over individuals. The condo association is a democratic governance mechanism and rules adopted by the majority must be followed by the minority until they are changed. Restrictions on the use of common areas enable people to enjoy the aesthetics of

---

2. John Rawls, *Justice as Fairness: A Restatement* (Erin Kelly ed. 2001).
3. City of Ladue v. Gilleo, 512 U.S. 43 (1994).

living in a built environment with uniform appearance. Everyone benefits if we allow people to create that kind of housing. The law should promote the liberty of individuals to create such peaceful and beautiful environments by promoting this type of property right. That can only be done by ensuring that individual owners have obligations to comply with rules adopted by the majority of their neighbors.

The world is better off allowing that form of housing to exist. Such a world does not require anyone to live in a condo; it merely makes the option possible. If we did not know whether we wanted to live in such housing or not, the question would be whether we should allow it to be created. Answering "yes" to that question enlarges our options and allows people to sort themselves into different kinds of housing environments. Just as you have the right to buy and live in a single-family home not regulated by a condo association, so others have the right to create and live in such environments. Don't stop someone from having choices about the kind of housing they want if you would want to be able to choose the kind of housing you want.

§11.3 Coherence & reflective equilibrium

Lawyers navigate competing values and rights in the context of rules and principles established in precedents and statutes. They sometimes start with principles and rules and use those to make sense of decided cases. Other times, they focus on the results in decided cases and seek to generate rules and principles from them. When a new case does not easily fit prior rules and cases, we may need to tweak one or the other so the new case fits in the system and we are happy that the existing set of rules and cases makes sense. Sometimes we reason from the top down (rules to cases) and sometimes from the bottom up (cases to rules). We stop when we have done the best we can.

Philosopher John Rawls called back and forth analysis "reflective equilibrium."[4] On one hand, we reason from general principles and rules down to specific cases (deduction). For example, we embrace fundamental norms like dignity, liberty, and equality and we make judgments about how to specify what those values mean in the context of concrete disputes.

On the other hand, we reason from the bottom up by focusing on strong

---

4. John Rawls, *Justice as Fairness: A Restatement* 29–32 (Erin Kelly ed. 2001).

intuitions about how specific cases should be decided. We treat those cases as fixed points; they may be precedents we are sure we do not want to overrule or they may be strong intuitions about how certain moral quandaries should be resolved in specific cases. We relate those fixed cases to general principles (induction). For example, we know that homeowners have the constitutional right to fly the American flag and that local governmental zoning laws that prohibit this are unconstitutional. We also know that condo associations have the right to regulate the appearance, color, and architectural features of common areas in a condominium building. We take those fixed precedents as a given and try to formulate governing principles that justify them and that distinguish them from each other.

The method of reflective equilibrium requires us to reason back and forth from principles to cases, and from cases to principles. We revise one or the other until we have a set of principles and cases we can support and justify. Hard cases do not easily fit within prior rules and cases because we are not sure how to classify them. When we consider a hard case, we reason back and forth between cases and principles with the goal of developing a coherent story of how they all fit together. This requires the decision maker to fuse available normative and legal resources in the best possible manner, given the context within which she is acting.

Reason top down from principles and norms to specific cases (deduction)

Reason bottom up from intuitions about specific cases to generate general principles or norms that support those case intuitions (induction)

Then fit a hard case into existing principles and existing cases

Either by amending the principles to fit our strong intuitions about specific cases

Or move cases from one side of the line to the other to fit them with our strong intuitions about governing principles

The common law system contains both rules and principles and precedents that show how those rules and principles apply in specific cases. A case is hard when it arguably fits within multiple categories, principles, norms, or rules. When multiple normative arguments are relevant, competing and contested institutional roles are present, and values are conflicting but powerful, we simply have to do the best we can.

Reflective equilibrium does not operate wholly deductively or inductively, and it does not follow a strict decision procedure. Nor does it resolve all value conflicts by an algorithmic metatheory. Analysis can deductively begin from the top down by applying principles to particular cases. Or it can inductively begin from the bottom up by focusing on our strong intuitions about how to resolve specific cases and then crafting principles that make sense of those intuitions.

The goal is to interpret and revise either the principles or the case results so that we have a combination that we can accept and defend and that provide as coherent a system of principles and applications as is possible for us to create. Coherence does not mean mathematical precision but consistency appropriate to moral and legal choices that recognize the pull of competing values and norms. Aristotle taught us that ethics is not an exact science; any assertions about right and wrong can only have "as much clarity as the subject matter allows."[5] At the same time, that does not mean that we cannot try to make our principles and cases fit together in a system of justification that makes sense and that we can defend and accept.

If we start from the top down, we focus on values, norms, principles, rules of law, and legal doctrines and try to see how they apply to the case at hand. If we start from the bottom up, we focus on specific cases where we have applied the law in the past. We identify fact situations that are on both sides of the line and about which there is no disagreement or about which we have settled intuitions. We identify cases in the middle (including the one we need to decide) that are problematic and hard, either because they seem to infringe on important values or because we have not been able to generate a good reason why they belong on one side of the fence rather than the other.

A combination of analogy and policy arguments helps divide the cases that are appropriately governed by one rule or another. We use factual and normative similarities among cases to explain how we are treating like cases alike, and what makes them alike or different. We combine those factual discussions with attention to principle and policy that can legitimately distinguish the cases in which a rule applies and those in which it does not apply. We search for the appropriate analogies to the case before us and the right mix of values and principles that can justify the resulting legal rule structure and outcomes in specific cases. The result may not be a set of principles that can be applied in a purely logical manner because attention to social context, historical settlement of issues, and judicial role consider-

---

5. Aristotle, *Ethics* 5 (John Warrington trans. & ed., J.M. Dent & Sons Ltd. 1963).

ations all matter. The method of reflective equilibrium works within a tradition and requires exercise of practical reason and considered judgment.

Our condo owner acknowledges that under current law the First Amendment does not apply to decisions of private entities like condo associations. At the same time, he argues that free speech is a fundamental right and that the common law of property and contract should be interpreted or modified to give condo unit owners the same right to fly the American flag as is enjoyed by owners of single-family homes that are not subject to rules of a homeowners association. He acknowledges that condo associations generally have the right to govern common property but seeks a limited exemption for owners exercising their right to engage in free speech. He may claim only a right to fly the American flag or a broader right to post signs that express messages. Either way, he will suggest that we can reconcile the right of condo associations to govern common property with the free speech rights of unit owners by creating a limited exception to the condo rules for expressive speech that does not interfere with the use and enjoyment of neighboring property.

The condo association will argue that there is a reason why the First Amendment applies only to state action. In the private sphere, people should be free to shape their environment as they wish. Anyone who takes a job or becomes a member of a religious organization or becomes a student at a university becomes subject to the rules the organization sets. Organizations cannot exist without rules that ensure that its members do their jobs, treat others in the organization respectfully, and interact with customers or members of the public in a manner that furthers the goal of the institution. It is a key aspect of human liberty to empower individuals to create associations and to govern themselves through rules they freely choose. Those rules include limitations on speech.

That means that there is a reason that private associations are not subject to constitutional limitations. Condo associations have the right to limit expressive conduct in common areas because the members want to live in an environment that is peaceful, respectful, and comfortable for their members. While you cannot escape regulation by government, you can choose not to be subject to rules of a condo association simply by living elsewhere. When you buy property that includes areas commonly owned by others and governed by them, you are agreeing to abide by rules promulgated by the governing body. You are free to try to change those rules by convincing a majority in the association to amend them, but absent that you have agreed to be bound by those rules. Limits on your expressive freedom actually promote your liberty by enabling you and others to benefit from individual ownership of your apartment and common ownership of the rest of the building. You cannot accept the benefits of condo living without accepting the burdens.

SUMMARY OF JUSTIFICATION TECHNIQUES

JUSTIFICATION

Framing

- Background understandings
- Framing the issue
- Storytelling

Value Specification & Contextualization

- Asserting & specifying values
- Social context & restrained interpretation of values

Prioritization

- Balancing interests
- Golden Rule, social contract, reasons we can accept
- Coherence & reflective equilibrium

PART 5

Examples

This part contains three examples of persuasive normative argument about what the law should be in three different contexts. They are presented in the form of judicial opinions deciding particular factual and legal disputes. All three are variations of real cases, with some of the facts altered. I have taken the liberty of beginning by arguing for the result that, after careful deliberation, I personally have come to favor, presenting it as the "majority opinion," followed by a dissenting opinion where I try to articulate the best arguments for an alternative rule of law.

If these were real judicial opinions, they would also discuss existing sources of law, whether statutes, regulations, or common law precedents and would interpret and apply them. If the source of law were a statute or regulation, the focus would be on interpreting the text of those laws and the policies they were intended to serve. If the source were the common law, there would be discussion about the rules previously adopted by the courts in that jurisdiction and explanation of whether this case is covered by an existing rule, whether it is a case of first impression that needs to be resolved in a manner consistent with other persisting rules of law, and whether an existing rule needs to be reinterpreted, limited, extended, or modernized (even overruled) to accord with contemporary values and changes in background statutes and regulations.

Rather than focus on interpreting applicable sources of law, these mock opinions focus on normative arguments about what the law should be, especially arguments about justice and fairness and arguments about social welfare. In each opinion, I frame the issue, tell the story, and then make normative arguments—on both sides—about fairness, social welfare, predictability, and statutory or constitutional interpretation. I try then to give reasons why one set of considerations should prevail over the other. Each side's argument acknowledges the arguments on both sides and present reasons—justifications— for going one way rather than the other. Rather than separate the framing techniques and arguments analytically, I try to meld them together to present the best justification I can for going one way or another. At the same time, you can see the framing techniques by focusing on how each opinion states what the issue is, and you can see storytelling techniques by the way the facts are presented.

The arguments I make are not the only possible ones that could be made; these examples are given only to help illustrate how persuasive argument can encompass and combine various techniques and values, while acknowledging complexity and the fact that the case is hard, while trying to give reasons that could or should be accepted by the losing side.

CHAPTER 12.

Property

Access to your own land

OPINION FOR THE COURT. A landowner named Tom Green owns a parcel of land completely surrounded by land owned by others.[1] Since he bought the lot, he has been getting to his land over private roads that traverse the lands of two of his neighbors. Those neighbors gave him oral permission to use their private roads to get from his land to public roads and back again. However, after many years of using those private roads, both neighbors have revoked permission to use them and have put gates blocking access to their lands. The only other way Green can get to a public road from his land (or to his land from a public road) is by way of a private road that goes to the north of Green's land over a parcel owned by Emma Brown. Brown is the woman who sold Green's land to him in the first place, and she did so on the understanding Green would not be crossing her remaining land to get to a public road.

The question in this case is: does an owner have the right to get to his own land? The answer is "yes." Owners have no right to sell a landlocked parcel; if you sell land with no access to a public road, you must give the buyer the right to cross your remaining land to reach a public way. The common law in many jurisdic-

---

1. This hypo is a variation on the case of Finn v. Williams, 33 N.E. 2d 226 (Ill. 1941).

tions recognizes an "easement by necessity."[2] An easement is a permanent right to a specific use of land owned by another, often encompassing a right of way or passage for utility lines. Most easements are created by agreement, but when an owner sells his backyard to another without providing for a right to cross the remaining land of the seller to get to a public road, the law grants such a right to the buyer on the assumption that no one would buy land if they had no way to get to it. An "easement by necessity" is deemed to be an implied term in the agreement.

The rule is designed to promote the will of the parties. When the formal written documents do not contain such an easement, the parties likely intended one to exist. Otherwise the buyer would be paying money for land that he has no ability to use or benefit from and people do not usually pay good money and get nothing in return.

The rule is also based on considerations of justice and policy. A seller who intends to sell land without granting a right to get to it is taking money on false pretenses, knowing the buyer believes access will be allowed while the seller intends to deny that very access. Consumer protection laws ensure that sellers do not engage in unfair or deceptive business practices, and it would be a kind of fraud to sell something the buyer intends to use while depriving the buyer of any ability to use it.

Access to otherwise landlocked property also serves the public interest. Land that cannot be used will be left idle, depriving both the owner and the public of the benefits of that land. Because land is a scarce resource, taking land out of circulation harms the public unless the land is devoted to socially beneficial purposes, such as conservation.

Even if one might imagine selling property to someone who has no way to get to it, the law should only find such a result, if at all, when the sales contract or deed formally waives the buyer's right to passage over remaining land of the seller to get to a public way, and we are sure that is what the buyer intended.

While it is true that the Statute of Frauds requires all agreements about property to be in writing to be enforceable, the courts have long created exceptions to that rule to avoid injustice. Judges have an obligation to enforce statutes, but we are also obligated to define the factual situations to which

---

2. An "easement" is a limited right to use someone else's land. Examples include rights of way (rights to use a road crossing someone else's land) or utility easements (rights to place telephone wires across the property of another).

statutes apply. Since equity courts in England altered the common law to achieve just results in specific cases, courts have had equitable powers to craft results to avoid injustice. Just as the New York legislature never intended to allow a grandson to kill his grandfather to stop him from changing his will, so our legislature would not have wanted the Statute of Frauds to allow a seller to sell property while denying the buyer any access to the very property for which the seller was accepting money. That is why courts in every state have adopted the doctrine of easement by necessity and why legislatures have accepted that common law rule without amending their statutes to get rid of it.

The doctrine of easement by necessity is a predictable rule of law even though it grants rights not reduced to writing in the sales contract or deed. Those who sell a parcel of their own land that is not located on a public road know they must grant the buyer a right to cross their remaining land to get to a public road. While defining the scope of that easement would be easier if the parties had reduced it to writing, the rule is predictable enough to guide conduct and expectations. The opposite rule may be more predictable (no easement of access unless the deed to the buyer creates one) but any gains in predictability that rule would create are more than offset by the costs to society of making land inaccessible and by the unfairness of selling property while preventing the owner from accessing the property. When one sells a car, for example, the law gives the buyer a right to enter land of the seller to take possession of the car. Otherwise, the seller could take money for the car and never hand it over. The same principle applies here.

This case, however, differs from the usual case because, at the time the buyer bought the land, he had alternative ways to get to the property. Moreover, at the time of the purchase, seller Brown communicated to Green that she did not want to sell the parcel to Green if he would be using the road over her property. Buyer Green told seller Brown that he would not need to do that since the neighbors were accommodating him with access over their lands. Brown had no intention of selling Green land that he could not get to; both parties assumed that permission to use the neighboring lands would continue since Green was buying the parcel based on oral assurances by the neighbors that he could use their roads. While it would have been wise to get those promises in writing by buying easements across one or both of those parcels, Green failed to do so, relying on the good will of the neighbors and trusting them to provide the access he needed to get to the land he was buying.

The fact that the parties to the sale discussed whether the buyer would be able to traverse the seller's land makes this case different from prior cases. Because of alternative means of access, a reasonable buyer might well have intended to buy the land even though he had no right to traverse the private road over the grantor's remaining land. The question in this case is therefore whether such a buyer should have the right to cross remaining land of the seller once other permissive rights of entry have been revoked by neighbors who had no obligation, at the time the parcels were severed from each other, to grant him the right to use their private roads.

Green argues that these facts do not require a different result in this case. The same fairness and policy concerns that apply in the core fact situation covered by the doctrine of easement by necessity apply here.

First, an owner has the right to get to his own land. It is inconsistent with the concept of ownership to be deprived of any ability to use what you own in any way or to be denied access to it. A buyer expects to be able to use what he is buying unless the object is a dangerous controlled substance or an environmental law prohibits development of the land. A seller who sells his backyard should not be allowed to do so unless ownership of the backyard comes with a right to cross the front yard to get to the back.

When a driveway or road already exists linking the front to the otherwise landlocked backyard, the right should be defined by the entitlement to use the existing driveway or road to get to the land the buyer has purchased. This result is fair to the seller because he has no right to take someone's money and give them nothing in return. A reasonable seller would know that the buyer was buying not just paper ownership of the backyard, or the right to exclude the seller from building on it, but a right to use the land himself. The fact that access was possible across neighboring lands is irrelevant. Those owners had no duty to provide such access. If the seller was relying on the continued availability of those means of access, she should have insisted upon written proof of agreements with one or both neighbors. Only then could she be secure that the buyer would not need to cross her land to get access to a public road. She has no right to sell land that is inaccessible.

Not only does Green have a right to get to his land, but he has a right to sell it. However, land is not alienable (no one will buy it) if there is no way to get to it. A lack of access makes the property useless to any prospective buyer. The only possible buyers would be neighboring owners. There is no guarantee that any of them wants his land. If they did, then they might compete with each other to offer a reasonable purchasing price. But seeking offers from three or four potential buyers is far different from selling the property on the open market. With so few potential purchasers, the owner is likely to get very little money for the land. Moreover, if the neighbors induced him to buy the parcel by giving him assurances that he would be able to get to it via roads on their lands, and they subsequently have revoked that access, then they have acted in a quasi-fraudulent manner and unfairly induced Green to rely on their assurances in reasonably investing in buying the parcel because of them. The hard feelings, and the lack of value of a landlocked parcel, may complicate negotiations and prevent the sale of the land to any of the neighbors. While the land is transferable in theory, it may be nontransferable in practice because of impediments to transacting. The land may therefore remain landlocked, both unusable and nontransferable in the marketplace. That will take the land out of circulation and deprive the public of its benefits.

Society would be better off if owners had the ability to access and use their own land. A seller who does not want the buyer to cross the road on her land is free to keep the parcel rather than sell it. Granting access across remaining land of the seller maximizes the joint fair market value of the parcels and creates a fair distribution of the benefits and burdens of land ownership. If the seller really values the right to be free from having Green cross her road more than he values the right to use it, she can offer him enough money to induce him to relinquish his rights—probably by buying the land back from him. Because she has no right to stop him from getting to the land she sold him, it is appropriate to place the burden on her to buy the parcel back from Green rather than putting the onus on him to either sell the property back to her at a low price or to live with ownership but no ability to access his own land.

We are confident that the result we find in this case is consistent with legislative policy, fair to both parties, and good for society.

DISSENTING OPINION #1. While the doctrine of easement by necessity is both fair and wise, it should not be extended to a case where the parties discussed the question of access and resolved it by not granting the buyer a right to cross remaining lands of the seller. To do so is to rewrite the contract and give the buyer something he did not bargain for. The question in this case is: why should we give an easement to a buyer who did not bargain for one? If he wanted it, why didn't he bargain for it? He took a risk that permissive access to neighboring lands would continue. But those grants of permission were not promises, and they were never reduced to writing as the Statute of Frauds requires. While the doctrine of easement by necessity promotes the probable intent of the parties when they have not discussed the issue, it cannot fulfill that function in a case where the parties actually talked about the problem of access and the buyer agreed to forego paying for the right to cross the seller's land.

The majority opinion argues that owners have a right to get to their property. However, so do owners have the right to exclude nonowners from their land. In this case, Brown refused to sell an easement over her own land and Green bought her backyard knowing that. He has no right to something she refused to sell. We should not rewrite the contract to obtain the result we think he should have bargained for. He knew what he was doing. He took a risk and it did not pan out. It is not our job to protect him from his own mistakes nor to force Brown to give up property rights against her will. We do not force an owner to sell her land to a prospective buyer even if that buyer offers far more than its fair market value. She has the right to refuse to sell at any price. We should not force her to sell an easement she does not want to sell just to help someone whose predicament is of his own making.

Society benefits when parties to land transactions are free to shape them in ways that benefit both parties. While easements by necessity generally are fair to both parties and beneficial to society, the opposite is true when the parties actually refuse to agree to create such easements. If Brown had known that the sale of the land to Green meant that he would be crossing her road, she might not have sold him the land at all. There is no reason not to allow the sale of the backyard when the buyer was content with permissive access over neighboring land owned by strangers to his deed. By making access to one's land over the seller's land a mandatory term in land contracts for landlocked parcels, the majority refuses to allow contracts with different terms to be made. The costs of rewriting the agreement in this case outweigh the benefits. Those costs include preventing certain kinds of mutually beneficial and socially harmless arrangements.

Nor is it true that the land is completely inalienable because there would be no buyers for a landlocked parcel. The land might very well be bought by someone who also bought one of the surrounding parcels. That would enable access to the land without forcing Brown to sell an easement she has no interest in selling. The most likely buyers are one of the neighbors, as the majority explains, but that does not mean that the property will fetch an unfair price. After all, the price was initially premised on the fact that there was no deeded easement of access. That should have depressed the value of the land. If Green wants to sell the land now because he has no way to get to it, it is likely he can sell it to one of his neighbors. If the neighbors are offering a low price, that is because Green probably bought the land for a low price, given the fact that it was otherwise landlocked. In any event, the only impediment to sale is Green himself. There will very likely be some price at which a neighbor would be happy to take the deed away from Green. The fact that he may lose money on the deal is his own fault.

An owner has the right to get to his own land unless he agrees otherwise. In this case, he did agree otherwise, and so no easement across the land of Emma Brown should be granted.

DISSENTING OPINION #2. Green should be denied the right to an easement by necessity, not because it is acceptable to have a landlocked parcel, but because the neighbors who gave him permission to cross their lands have no right to revoke their permission if he invests substantially in reliance on their permission and they are aware that he was likely to do so.

The neighbors gave Green oral permission to cross their lands knowing that he would not have bought a landlocked parcel unless he was able to use their roads. Permission to access someone else's land is called a "license." Licenses are normally revocable at will. "Easements," in contrast, are permanent rights to use or cross someone else's land. While the Statute of Frauds generally requires that easements be in writing, the common law doctrine of "easement by estoppel" changes a revocable license into an irrevocable easement when the licensee reasonably relies on the license and invests in buying or improving land on the basis of that license. That is what happened here.

There is no need for Green to cross the land of Brown; he already owns easements over the lands of his other two neighbors who should not be allowed to revoke their permission to use their roads once he bought the land in reliance on his ability to use those roads. To let them revoke their permission would be to allow them to commit a kind of fraud. While they made no written promise, they said "yes" when asked if he could use their roads, knowing he was likely to rely on their statement in his decision to buy the land. That "yes" cannot later become a "no" without violating Green's reasonable, investment-backed expectations.

CHAPTER 13.

Torts & Contracts

Fraudulent transactions

OPINION OF THE COURT. Two Massachusetts residents negotiated and signed an agreement in Massachusetts for the sale of
a small business (a hardware store) located in New Hampshire,
along with the building and land on which it sits.[1] In the course
of the negotiations, seller John Blue made oral representations
to buyer Sally Red about the profitability of the business and
showed the buyer accounting books that supposedly confirmed
those facts.

Those representations turned out to be false. The books shown
to the buyer were fabricated and contained inaccurate figures.
The buyer relied on those representations in deciding to go ahead
with the purchase of the business and the land. After signing the
sales agreement in Massachusetts, the closing took place in New
Hampshire with the seller conferring the real estate deed to the
buyer and the buyer paying the agreed-upon purchase price. The
business was similarly sold by a mutually signed agreement.

After the sale, the buyer discovered the fraud and sued the
seller in state court in Massachusetts seeking (a) rescission of the

---

1. This hypo is a variation on the case of Danann Realty Corp. v. Harris,
157 N.E.2d 597 (N.Y. 1959). The state laws about both torts and contracts are
fabricated for the purpose of constructing an illustrative case.

agreement (returning the land and building and business to the seller) and (b) damages for the tort of fraud.

The seller admits the fraud but argues that the buyer waived any rights to return the property she purchased or to sue for damages for fraud because the sales agreement signed in Massachusetts contained a "non-reliance clause" by which both parties agreed that they were not relying on any representations not included in the written agreement itself.

New Hampshire law is on the defendant seller's side while Massachusetts law favors the plaintiff buyer. Under New Hampshire law, a contract that contains an "as is" clause whereby buyer buys the product as is without any representations by the seller about its quality or condition other than those written in the contract is fully enforceable even if the seller made oral statements that are not true to induce the buyer to buy the object. A non-reliance clause similarly amounts to a promise by the buyer that she is not relying on any representations not contained in the agreement; such clauses are fully enforceable in New Hampshire.

A claim of fraud requires proof of false statements intended to deceive and to induce the buyer to rely on those statements, plus reasonable reliance by the buyer on the false statements to the detriment of the buyer. While contracts can be rescinded if one party commits fraud, that rule does not apply if the elements necessary to prove fraud are missing.

New Hampshire law is based on the premise that either party may make statements that the other party may misunderstand. Further, after sale, either party may regret what they have done. Nonreliance clauses protect both parties from false claims by the other side. This case involves a claim that the seller lied to the buyer. But it is equally possible to envision a case where the buyer lies about what the seller said to the buyer. A buyer who is remorseful about the deal and wants to get out of it may attempt to do so by claiming the seller made statements on which the buyer relied, even if the seller said no such thing, or spoke but meant no such thing. Massachusetts law is more worried about lies told by the seller, giving the buyer a way to rescind such a deal, but New Hampshire law is more worried about lies the buyer told to slink out of the deal that the buyer regrets. New Hampshire law also seeks to protect sellers from misunderstandings by the buyer through giving buyers incentives to put into writing representations they think the seller made upon which the buyer is relying.

New Hampshire law is fair to the buyer in this case. Since the buyer promised that she was not relying on any statements or representations not included in the written documents when she entered the agreement, it is unreasonable for her to rely on external representations, whether written or oral. If the buyer wanted to rely on external representations, she could have put them into the contract so the parties both would understand the nature of the promises each was making. Because she did not, under New Hampshire law, she cannot get damages for being harmed by relying on a false statement. This rule protects sellers (and buyers) from unfair surprise.

New Hampshire law also promotes the sale of land and businesses by inducing contracting parties to negotiate to make clear what their mutual expectations are. If representations are important enough to rely on, they are important enough to include in the agreement. Using the written agreement to define the rights and obligations of the parties will ensure that the parties are attuned to the nature of the agreement and will keep cases out of court that are of the "he said/she said" variety. This will promote the alienability of land and businesses, decrease the costs of transactions, lower the administrative costs of deciding cases in court, and clarify what parties can expect from business negotiations.

Massachusetts law, in contrast, provides that contracting parties cannot protect themselves from fraud claims by artful language in an agreement. Fraud vitiates and makes a mockery of consent. Contracts are enforced because they represent a "meeting of the minds," but that is not possible when one of the parties is lying to induce the other to think she is buying something other than what she actually is buying. Allowing the seller to make statements intending to induce the buyer to rely on them, and then attempting to disable the buyer from rescinding the deal by including a nonreliance clause in the contract, would allow the seller to get away with fraudulently stealing the buyer's hard-earned dollars. Nonreliance clauses clarify what the agreement is about; they do not give anyone a free pass to defraud others. For that reason, under Massachusetts law, the buyer can bring a claim for fraud and obtain damages for the resulting harm and can rescind the agreement, return title to the land and building to the seller, along with ownership of the business.

Massachusetts law protects people from fraud. Fraud is a form of theft because it enables someone to take someone else's money under false pretenses by getting them to pay for something and then not giving it to them. Massachusetts wants to promote voluntary market transactions but not to allow people to take property belonging to someone else without their free and voluntary consent. Legal rules that protect people from fraud encourage them to engage in market transactions by enabling them to trust others. Those rules also protect market participants from the need to negotiate very long agreements that list every single representation each party is relying on to justify the transaction.

The question is: which law should apply? The answer depends on how we see the case. Is this a case about the sale of a New Hampshire business? If so, both parties could anticipate application of New Hampshire law. Is this a case instead of one Massachusetts resident picking the pocket of another Massachusetts resident while in their home state? If so, the law of the place of the wrong (Massachusetts) should apply.

This is a multistate transaction with significant contacts in two states. Both states have significant interests in applying their law and both parties have legitimate claims to the protection of each state's law. However, the relative weight of state interests and party rights differs on the two legal issues.

As to the question of whether the buyer should be able to rescind the deal and give back the property, New Hampshire law should apply. New Hampshire has greater interests than does Massachusetts in regulating the sale of New Hampshire real estate and businesses. It has the best claim to govern the way real estate transactions occur within its borders and Massachusetts should refrain from extending its regulations to interfere with New Hampshire's ability to regulate its own land titles and real estate sales. Nor is that result unfair to the buyer, who was on notice that the subject matter of the transaction was located in New Hampshire. The Massachusetts buyer knew that she was stepping across the border to do business, and she takes the obligations, as well as the rights, of the law of the state she entered to do business. That means the buyer may not rescind the deal; title to the land and ownership of the business remain with the buyer.

However, on the question of whether the buyer can sue the seller for damages for fraud, for lost profits and other financial loss occasioned because of the fraud, that issue should be governed by Massachusetts law. The buyer has a right to the protection of Massachusetts law when she contracts there and is defrauded there by another Massachusetts resident, and application of Massachusetts law will not cause any unfair surprise to the seller. While New Hampshire has the stronger interest in regulating sales of New Hampshire land, Massachusetts has the greater interest in deciding whether the victim of a fraud perpetrated in Massachusetts should have a remedy for that fraud. On this issue, there is no unfairness to the defendant to have Massachusetts law apply. A tort committed inside Massachusetts that harms a Massachusetts resident should be governed by Massachusetts law regardless of the location of the property being transferred. While Massachusetts should defer to New Hampshire to allow it to govern the contract and property aspects of this case, New Hampshire should defer to Massachusetts to allow it to govern the tort claim. Just as the buyer knew she was crossing the border to buy property in New Hampshire, the seller knew he was crossing the border to commit fraud against a Massachusetts resident at home where her home state law protects her from such wrongful conduct.

The defendant prevails on the contract issue; title to the land remains with plaintiff buyer as does ownership of the business, as New Hampshire law requires. The plaintiff wins on the tort issue; the plaintiff is entitled to damages under Massachusetts law for costs resulting from the seller's fraudulent statements and conduct.

CONCURRING IN PART AND DISSENTING IN PART #1. The majority opinion appears Solomonic, but appearances can deceive. The issues can be distinguished only if they are not inextricably linked. Massachusetts law should apply on both questions because it makes no sense to find that a fraud was committed and then deny the buyer appropriate remedies for the fraud. The buyer correctly argues that Massachusetts law should apply on both issues because she has a right to be protected under the law of her home state while contracting at home. Nor can this be unfair to the seller who knew he was contracting in Massachusetts with another Massachusetts resident. He has no right to hide behind New Hampshire law while committing a wrong in Massachusetts.

Massachusetts interests in applying its law should prevail over those of New Hampshire in this case. New Hampshire may have strong interests in regulating New Hampshire transactions to promote the marketability of New Hampshire land and businesses, but this transaction was not confined to New Hampshire. While it makes sense for a Massachusetts court generally to apply New Hampshire law to New Hampshire transactions, New Hampshire should defer to Massachusetts to allow it to remedy wrongful conduct that harms one of its residents as the result of conduct inside the state by another resident. Even if this infringes on New Hampshire policy and interferes with an agreement to buy a New Hampshire business, most such transactions will be confined to New Hampshire and have the benefit of New Hampshire rules. So the cost to New Hampshire of applying Massachusetts law is low while the cost to Massachusetts of denying a remedy under Massachusetts law is high.

Standing before the court are two Massachusetts residents, one of whom defrauded the other by false representations made while in the Commonwealth of Massachusetts. New Hampshire cannot reasonably complain if Massachusetts applies its law to regulate conduct within its borders to protect its own residents from harm caused by other Massachusetts residents. New Hampshire residents can avoid the application of Massachusetts law by refraining from fraudulent conduct or conducting negotiations and transactions within the state that protects the seller from fraud claims.

Massachusetts law gives the plaintiff a remedy for the tortious conduct committed against her in Massachusetts; she has the right not to be saddled with an unprofitable business and real estate that is worth far less than she thought it was. Massachusetts interests outweigh those of New Hampshire. To allow the seller to retain the land is to let him benefit from his fraud and to deprive the victim of a complete remedy. The baby cannot be cut in two.

The contract can be rescinded, and the plaintiff is entitled to damages for the fraudulent conduct of the defendant. The plaintiff wins on all issues.

CONCURRING IN PART AND DISSENTING IN PART #2. I agree with my colleague that one state's law should govern both issues, but I would apply New Hampshire law, not Massachusetts law, to both the tort and contract claims. This is not a case of New Hampshire residents stepping over the border to wreak havoc in Massachusetts. It is a case of a Massachusetts resident going to New Hampshire to buy a business. The buyer cannot be unfairly surprised that New Hampshire law applies to the sale of lands and businesses inside New Hampshire and the seller has the right to the benefits of New Hampshire law when the subject matter of the transaction is New Hampshire land and property. The tort claim arises out of the business negotiations for the purchase of New Hampshire land and a New Hampshire business, so the plaintiff would not be unfairly surprised that the transaction is subject to New Hampshire law.

Rather than New Hampshire deferring to Massachusetts, this is a case where Massachusetts should defer to New Hampshire because New Hampshire has very strong interests in regulating its own real estate markets and business sales. Allowing the buyer to get out of the deal and bring a claim for fraud could tie up the parties in court for years, make title to the land unmarketable (who will buy property when it is not clear who owns it?)

and increase the costs of New Hampshire business transactions. Both states want to protect the parties from fraud but have opposite strategies for how to do this. New Hampshire has the right to protect sellers from claims by buyers that they relied on oral or extracontractual statements that the seller may or may not have made. Given the strong interest of each state in regulating business transactions in their state, Massachusetts should acknowledge that New Hampshire law is the appropriate way to adjudicate the case.

The contract is enforceable; title to the property should remain with the buyer; no remedy for the fraud can be awarded. The defendant wins on all issues.

CHAPTER 14.

Civil Rights

Sexual orientation discrimination & religious liberty

OPINION OF THE COURT. Does a baker have a constitutional right to violate a state public accommodation statute by refusing to design and sell a cake to a same-sex couple to celebrate their wedding anniversary when same-sex marriage violates the baker's religious beliefs?[1] State law in our jurisdiction prohibits discrimination on the basis of sexual orientation. Because the baker in this case, Joe Jones, would have designed and sold a cake to a male-female couple to celebrate their anniversary, but refused to do so for a male-male couple, and because of the close connection between same-sex marriage and sexual orientation, that refusal violated the state's antidiscrimination law. The sole issue is whether his constitutionally protected right to free exercise of religion gives him a right to be exempted from the state statute.

On one side is the shopkeeper who hopes to live his life in a way that affirms his religious convictions. He believes that if he designs and sells the cake, he is expressing support for what the cake celebrates—a same-sex marriage—and that is something his religion rejects. It was in 1962 that the Supreme Court

---

1. This case is a variation on the facts of Masterpiece Cakeshop, Ltd., v. Colo. Civil Rights Comm'n, 138 S. Ct. 1719 (U.S. 2017).

stopped public schools from forcing children to participate in prayers that may have been inconsistent with their religious beliefs or practices.[2] The Constitution prohibits coerced participation in a religious service; it does not allow the state to compel anyone to affirm a religious belief. The baker says this case is just like that.[3] Gay customers who want anniversary cakes can look elsewhere. The profit motive will induce someone to provide the service they seek. They can easily acquire what they need without imposing their religious views on the baker. Everyone wins under that solution.

On the other side, we have the couple: they want to shop in stores open to the public just like everyone else. They do not want to be treated like outcasts. They do not want to have to call ahead to see if they are welcome. They do not want to be excluded from stores because their religious beliefs are different from those of the shopkeeper. Neither homosexuality nor marriage violates their religious beliefs; indeed, their religion affirms their relationship. Like the baker, they seek to live their lives true to themselves and to their religious and moral commitments. The shopkeeper has a rightful claim to religious liberty but do so his customers.

Moreover, the cake will celebrate their anniversary. The anniversary cake expresses nothing about the baker, his beliefs, his religion, or his views. He may oppose same-sex marriage for religious reasons, but if he would design and make an anniversary cake for anyone, he must also do it for this couple. Nor does this constitute participation in a religious ceremony or compelled speech; rather, the refusal to design and sell the cake discriminates against the customers both on the basis of their religion and their sexual orientation. The baker opened a shop that sells cakes to the public and this couple is part of the public.

If the baker can exclude customers because their "lifestyle" violates his religious beliefs, does that mean that storeowners can refuse service to people of different religions? Both federal law and state statutes in forty-five states prohibit discrimination against customers on the basis of religion. Does a storeowner have the right to discriminate against Christians? Jews? Muslims? If the sale of a product to a customer constitutes an affirmation

---

2. Engel v. Vitale, 370 U.S. 421 (1962).

3. For the Supreme Court's most recent affirmation of this principle, *see* Janus v. American Federation of State, County, and Municipal Employees (AFSCME), 2018 WL 3129785 (U.S. 2018).

that the seller agrees with the buyer's religious views, does sale of an anniversary cake to a Jewish couple mean repudiation of Christ?

Does the seller have a right to refuse to design and sell a cake to an interracial couple because that violates his religious beliefs? The Supreme Court effectively answered that question in the negative in *Newman v. Piggie Park Enterprises*[4] when a restaurant owner refused to seat African American customers because of his religious beliefs that people of different races should not eat together in public. Just like our baker, that restaurant owner claimed that complying with a public accommodations law violated his religious beliefs and would, in effect, voice support for racial integration contrary to his own religious, political, and personal commitments. If religion were a defense to the 1964 federal public accommodation law, then racial segregation would have continued in the South. It is not possible to achieve the social benefits that civil rights laws provide if religious dissenters are free to ignore them.

Storeowners should not be free to discriminate against Christians. But if that is true, then Christians should not be free to discriminate against non-Christians. The baker claims that he is not discriminating "because of" the buyer's religion but because he cannot be forced to do anything that indicates support for conduct that violates his religious beliefs. Yet his willingness to design and sell wedding and anniversary cakes to Jewish couples suggests that such cakes do not, in general, constitute a religious act or participation in a religious exercise or express support for the customer's religious practices or beliefs. Nor should stores be free to discriminate against him because of his religion if he approaches them as a customer.

The baker is, of course, free to limit his cakes to Christians, if he does so in the right way. He can do that creating a nonprofit or a religious organization whose goals are limited to serving Christians. He can do that by giving cakes away as gifts. He can do that by refraining from operating a public accommodation. If your religion requires dealing only with others of your faith, you can do so by operating as a nonprofit religious entity and not offering goods to the general public. Because the interest in religious freedom is as fundamental as the interest in freedom from a racial caste system—and because same-sex couples have as much right to religious

---

4. Newman v. Piggie Park Enterprises, 256 F. Supp. 941, 945 (D.S.C. 1966), *aff'd in relevant part and rev'd in part on other grounds*, 377 F.2d 433 (4th Cir. 1967), *aff'd and modified on other grounds*, 390 U.S. 400 (1968).

liberty as do bakers—religious belief of the storeowner cannot justify an exemption from antidiscrimination laws.

Allowing anyone to assert religious beliefs as a way to violate a statute they do not like would make it impossible to have effective law enforcement. A society devoted to freedom of religion benefits from the rule of law; religious freedom does not include the right to ignore duly enacted statutes that are neutral with regard to religion and which do not compel people to worship or affirm beliefs against their will. And giving the baker a right to refuse service for religious reasons would deny customers the right to be served without regard to the customer's religion. Our society has chosen to privilege the religious freedoms of the customer over those of the seller so that everyone has access to the marketplace without exclusion, segregation, or discriminatory treatment.

As for going elsewhere, whether an alternative bakery is available depends on whether we are in a small town in the countryside or the big city, as well as how much prejudice there is locally against gay people. In a small town in a rural area, it may not be so easy to find these services elsewhere. More fundamentally, civil rights laws give people the freedom to enter businesses open to the public and to engage in commerce without having to find ones that are willing to deal with them. The whole point of public accommodations—and public accommodations law—is to make the marketplace open to people without invidious discrimination. The baker is entitled to believe that his refusal to design and sell the cake is not improperly discriminatory or invidious but the lawmaking body that makes that determination is our legislature. Giving storeowners a right to conscientiously object to civil rights laws would deprive those laws of any force. Their very point is to privilege access to public accommodations without discriminatory exclusion or second-class treatment and that right takes precedence over any claimed right of businesses to choose their customers in a discriminatory manner.

Public accommodation laws serve compelling government interests and those interests are sufficient to justify any incidental effect on religious sensibilities. Civil rights laws are designed to ensure equal access to the marketplace, to enable anyone to purchase goods and services regardless of their religion, and to prevent the creation of segregated markets. Any exemption granted in the public accommodation area cannot be confined to that context but would likely extend to employment, housing, and education. We would have Catholic and Protestant neighborhoods, Christian-only hotels, black and white neighborhoods, all-male workplaces, and universities free to allow or even promote sexual harassment of women. The government interest in keeping the marketplace open to all, without regard to race, religion, or sexual orientation is sufficient to justify a lack of exemptions for storeowners whose religious beliefs might cause them to deny services to members of protected groups.

Public accommodation laws also enable us to acquire property without discrimination. Human beings cannot flourish if we cannot acquire property. We also cannot flourish if we experience humiliating treatment when we interact with others in the marketplace or if we are segregated and treated as a subordinate caste. Therefore, we cannot flourish if shopkeepers are free to refuse to sell us property for discriminatory reasons. That rule protects Christians as well as non-Christians; it protects male-female couples as well as same-sex couples. Public accommodation laws preserve both religious liberty and access to property and the marketplace by ensuring that, no matter what your religion is, you can find a place to live, a place to work, and a place to shop. No one can be excluded from the marketplace because of who they are.

DISSENTING OPINION. The question in this case is not whether anyone can violate any law they like by uttering the magic word "religion." This case is about whether the state can coerce someone to express a belief contrary to his religion if he wants to participate in the marketplace on equal terms with others. The majority says that "no one can be excluded from the marketplace because of who they are." Doesn't that principle apply to business owners as well as customers? This case asks whether a business owner can be coerced to support a practice that he views as sinful; even more, it asks whether the owner can be compelled to commit a sin himself. The majority opinion overstates the interests of the customers and understates the interests of the baker. Neither the rule of law nor equal access to the market or freedom are at risk if we grant a limited exemption from a public accommodation law for religious dissenters. This issue in the case is specific and discrete. We are talking about whether someone can be compelled to express support for a marital relationship that violates his religious commitments. Our Constitution answers that question with a resounding "no."

The majority references the school prayer case. That case stands for the proposition that the state cannot force a person to engage in a religious act. Nor can the state compel someone to affirm religious beliefs that the person does not hold. What is and is not a religious act is not up to the state; it is up to each person who affirms a particular religious commitment or way of life. The majority suggests that "designing and selling a cake" does not constitute a religious act or make a statement of any kind, but it is the baker who has the right to say whether such a sale constitutes a religious act or not and whether it makes a statement that the baker cannot embrace.

Public accommodation laws guarantee equal access to goods and services, but they do not regulate what services businesses must provide. A store that prints words and symbols on T-shirts should not be required to create shirts with swastikas on them. Nor should it be required to sell shirts to those who intend to use them to promote a political party that the owner opposes. Songwriters routinely refuse to allow politicians to use their songs at rallies if they do not support those politicians. If they have the right to do that, then businesses have the right not to be compelled to create products that convey messages that the business finds offensive, especially if the owner considers the message to be religious in nature.

There is no evidence that we are facing the wide scale rebellion against civil rights laws that worries the majority. Most businesses are perfectly willing to sell goods and services to the general public. They are in business, after all, to make money, and refusing money offered to them by willing customers will soon put them out of business. If one owner is not willing to provide a good or services, others will do so. That is the magic of free competition. Moreover, since most stores are willing to design and sell goods to anyone, including wedding goods and anniversary cakes, access to the marketplace will be hardly limited at all if an exemption is provided to the seller in this case. That is especially true because the cases that have generated litigation have focused on marriage, which is both a civil and a religious act for many people.

Carving out a limited exemption from public accommodation laws for businesses that have sincere objections to particular messages will not suddenly result in apartheid or widespread discrimination on the basis of religion, race, or sexual orientation. While it is true that recent years have seen renewed discrimination against Jews and Muslims, as well as disturbing activity by white supremacists, the vast majority of large and small businesses remain open to the public without regard to race, religion, or sexuality. A limited exemption will simply give those few businesses that care about an issue the freedom to engage in business without violating their religious commitments while ensuring equal and dignified access to the marketplace for all.

In this case, neither party is asking to be left alone. Either the buyers have a right to force the seller to affirm a message that violates his religious beliefs, or the seller has a right to force the buyers to look elsewhere for their needs. The question is which legal rule is best able to protect the legitimate interests of both parties. Since most businesses will be open to the public without regard to religion or sexual orientation, and the buyers are likely to find another business willing to provide the same service, access to the marketplace is preserved. If that is so, then access to these services will not be limited in any significant way. While the customers may have suffered humiliation at being politely turned away, forced participation in compelled speech that violates one's religion imposes humiliation of another kind. It is possible to promote both religious freedom and equal protection of law without trampling on either. No business owner should be forced to affirm a belief they do not hold, unless the plaintiffs can show that they cannot obtain similar goods or services elsewhere.

CONCLUSION

There is no magic bullet you can use to change someone else's mind. That is especially true when an issue involves competing interests and values that stand in need of interpretation. But the first step in persuasion is to be sure that you know what you are talking about: have you thought carefully enough about the question? Have you listened to those who disagree with you? Have you considered arguments on the other side? What are they saying that is true? Only when you do that can you understand the claim you are making and what it means.

Persuasion about issues of public importance is not just about winning. It is about coming to see the ways in which the parties on both sides share certain fundamental values. It is those shared values that enable conversation to occur; it is those shared values that make persuasion a possibility. Recognizing those shared values also opens space for reasoned justification of a decision about what the law should be. It enables the decision maker to show understanding of the ways that a rule of law may affect legitimate interests of the losing party or others in society and to give reasons they could or should accept for living under that rule.

When judges decide hard cases, they have an obligation to be able to give reasons that could justify the result. If the case is really a hard one, the justification will have to recognize the legitimate interests of the losing side and explain why the concessions being asked of them are reasonable. This requires recognition of difference, but it also requires recognition of shared values. No argument will force the losing side to accept the loss, but requiring decision makers to give reasons does constrain their discretion and presses them to treat the losing side with dignity. The rule of law in a free and democratic society with government by, for, and of the people is a continuing task that each generation must undertake. Civil discourse and reasoned argument are the tools we use to do that work.

Checklist of Arguments

It is easy to focus on one argument or type of argument and give inadequate attention to others. It is very easy to ignore counterarguments and valid considerations on the other side. To help avoid these natural tendencies, here is a checklist of major arguments and counterarguments to consider making or thinking about when debating or deciding issues about what the law should be. They summarize the discussions in the chapters.

RIGHTS, FAIRNESS, JUSTICE

Interests & Values

- What interests does each person have?
- What values are served by protecting those interests?
- Why should those interests be protected and who has a duty to protect them?

Rights

Freedom of action   Security

Morality

Legitimate conduct   Wrongful conduct

Individualism   Altruism

Reasonable Expectations

- Did someone rely on actions or representations of another?
  - Was that reliance reasonable?
- Was the harm reasonably foreseeable?
- Would liability subject anyone to unfair surprise?

Fairness & Equality

- Is the action or rule fair to both parties?
- Does it treat each person with dignity?
- Does it treat each person with equal concern and respect?

Distributive Justice

- Does the rule create a fair distribution of the benefits and burdens of social life?
- Does a rule create an undue or disproportionate burden?

Liberty & Human Flourishing

- Does the rule promote liberty, meaning the right accommodation of freedom and security?
- Is the rule reasonable? Does it promote as appropriate concessions among free and equal persons?
- Does the rule enable each human being to flourish?

CONSEQUENCES, SOCIAL WELFARE, COSTS & BENEFITS

Social Welfare

- Which rule best promotes the general welfare?
- Which rule promotes social utility, happiness, or human flourishing?

Incentives

- What incentives do the alternative rules create?
- How will people behave if each rule is adopted?

Promotion of investment

- Which rule best promotes socially desirable economic investment?
- How does each rule stifle desirable development?
- Which rule best discourages socially harmful investment?

Cost Internalization

- Which rule best induces people to internalize the external costs of their activity?
- Which party should bear the burden of paying for the external costs of their conduct?

Cost-Benefit Analysis

- What are the costs and benefits of each rule?
- Which rule promotes the best overall outcome?

Transaction Costs

- Are the costs of bargaining high or low?
- If they are high should the law assign rights to the person who likely values them the most?
  - Or should the law attempt to lower transaction costs by making rights clear to promote bargaining?

Valuations

- Fair market value

- Auction (compare offer prices)

- Status quo (compare owner asking price to nonowner offer price)

- Redistribution (compare nonowner asking price to owner offer price)

- Reverse auction (compare asking prices)

Presumptions & Minimum Standards

- Is the agreement ambiguous or unambiguous?

  - If ambiguous,
    promote the intent of the parties

  - If ambiguous,
    promote public policy

- Does the arrangement impose harmful costs on third parties (externalities)?

- Does the agreement violate minimum standards for relationships in a free and democratic society that treats each person with equal concern and respect?

- If either answer is yes, should the agreement contain terms that are nonwaivable to protect third parties or ensure that people get what they are entitled to get out of the arrangement?

CASES & RULES

Precedent

- Apply precedent
- Distinguish precedent
- Reconcile conflicting precedents
- Overrule precedent

Rules & Standards

Rigid rules are predictable	Flexible standards allow justice in individual case
Rules are flexible	Standards are predictable

Interpretation

Formal, written sources alone to create legitimate expectations	Informal sources of expectation matter
Text is unambiguous	Text is ambiguous
If ambiguous, promote the will of the parties	If ambiguous, promote public policy

Democracy & the Rule of Law

Judicial restraint	Judicial activism
Defer to legislature to change the law	Modernize common law to accord with current legislation and evolving values
Legislative competence	Judicial competence

Framing

- Background understandings
- Framing the issue
- Storytelling

Value Specification & Contextualization

- Asserting & specifying values
- Social context & restrained interpretation of values

Prioritization

- Balancing interests
- Golden Rule, social contract, reasons we can accept
- Coherence & reflective equilibrium

FURTHER READING ON PERSUASION

Here is a selective list of books I have found helpful in my thinking about persuasion:

Michael Austin, *We Must Not Be Enemies: Restoring America's Civic Tradition* (2019)

Aristotle, *The Art of Rhetoric* (trans. H. C. Lawson-Tancred, Penguin ed. 2004).

Robert B. Cialdini, *Influence: The Psychology of Persuasion* (2007)(original 1984)

Marcus Tullius Cicero, *How to Win an Argument: An Ancient Guide to the Art of Persuasion* (James M. May ed. 2016)

Trish Hall, *Writing to Persuade* (2019)

Jay Heinrichs, *Thank You for Arguing: What Aristotle, Lincoln, and Homer Simpson Can Teach Us about the Art of Persuasion* (3d ed. 2017)

Steven Johnson, *Farsighted: How We Make the Decisions That Matter the Most* (2018)

Christopher McMahon, *Reasonableness and Fairness: A Historical Theory* (2016)

Susan Neiman, *Moral Clarity: A Guide for Grown-Up Idealists* (rev. ed. 2009)

Jedediah Purdy, *For Common Things: Irony, Trust, and Commitment in America Today* (1999)

Henry S. Richardson, *Practical Reasoning About Final Ends* 271 (1997)

Walter Sinnott-Armstrong, *Think Again: How to Reason and Argue* (2018)

Mark Timmons, *Morality Without Foundations: A Defense of Ethical Contextualism* (1998)

Joel P. Trachtman, *The Tools of Argument: How the Best Lawyers Think, Argue, and Win* (2013)

Ronald Waicukauski, Paul Mark Sandler &JoAnne Epps, *The 12 Secrets of Persuasive Argument* (2009)

Useful books that focus on arguments used in the context of answering law school exam questions are:

Barry Friedman & John C.P. Goldberg, *Open Book: Succeeding on Exams from the First Day of Law School* (2011)

Jeremy Paul, *Getting to Maybe: How to Excel on Law School Exams* (1999)